The Third Sex

Kathoey – Thailand's Lady oys

BY THE SAME AUTHOR
PUBLISHED BY SOUVENIR PRESS

Social Causes of Illness
Mind, Stress and Health

The Third Sex

Kathoey – Thailand's Ladyboys

Richard Totman

Souvenir Press

For the *kathoey* of Thailand

Contents

List of Illustrations

Appearing between pages 86–87.

Acknowledgements

I would like to thank these people for their help with my research: Dr Pichet Saiphan, Dr Sumitr Pitiphat, Dr Saran Wannachamras, Dr Preecha Tiewtranon, Dr Shalardchai, Mr Surasak Sudjai, Mr Sintoo Manprasong and and Vagn Pedersen. Also the libraries of SOAS in London, Nielson Hayes in Bangkok and the librarians of the Archives of the City of Brussels. I am most grateful to Felicity-Ann Hall, Helen Duncan, Pauline Sutton and Ben Foster for their help on a draft of this book.

Introduction

The first time I stayed in Thailand for an extended period, in 1998/9, I had no intention of travelling with my background as a social scientist in tow, but purely as a tourist. Ten years previously I had stopped off in Bangkok for four days on my way back from Taiwan and something about Thailand, its people and their way of life, arrested me even in that short space of time. Since then my return visits were to confirm the opinion shared by many travel writers that there is something strangely unique about the place. Some say it is to do with the fact that Thailand, or Siam as it used to be known, is the only country in south-east Asia that has resisted all attempts at colonisation. The resulting cultural continuity over the centuries might be expected to endow its people with a certain self-confidence. Not for nothing is Thailand known as 'The Land of Smiles'.

On 9 January 1999, the *Bangkok Post*, a daily broadsheet printed in English, carried a feature which caught my eye, entitled *Roses of the North: The Kathoey of Chiang Mai University*. On the front page was a picture of two attractive girls dressed in traditional Thai costumes. Or so I thought. The piece begins:

> Suwanna, an English teacher at Chiang Mai University, remembers being puzzled. 'The name on the roster said "Somsak", so I looked for a boy. Instead a beautiful girl raised her hand – it was quite a shock!'

The article goes on to describe a sorority of *kathoey* at the university, the tolerant atmosphere towards them and the varied but mostly accepting attitudes of the other students.

I showed the article to Helen, my travel companion at this time, who gave it a cursory look and said something along the lines, 'Yes, very pretty', then returned to her breakfast. When I pointed out that the people in the photographs were not ordinary girls she stared at me in disbelief, grabbed the paper and read the article through. We decided we must see these folk in the flesh, so we enquired about *kathoey* shows in the town and that night went to see one. These cabarets are variously described in the tourist press and in advertisements as 'drag shows', or 'transvestite cabaret'. However, it was immediately apparent that such descriptions are quite misleading. Here was no camp burlesque but something quite different, with no counterpart in the West; nothing even remotely comparable. We both sensed that behind the outwardly superficial entertainment and glitter lay something more serious and perhaps more deep-rooted. Could these performers and this cabaret show be a contemporary expression of an age old cultural tradition? And that was the beginning of my interest in this enigmatic microculture and the starting point of three years' research, with over a year of this time spent in Thailand.

Partly on account of my own commitment to a personal, interactive method of doing social research, and partly to do with good fortune, my account of *kathoey* in Thailand offered here does not take the form of a strict social-scientific study in the conventional sense. Rather it attempts to give a picture of the lives of these people and their place in Thai culture by spending as much time as possible with them and listening at length to what they have to say. My mentor and friend at Oxford, the Philosopher of Science Rom Harré, wrote a book entitled *The Explanation of Social Behaviour*. In this book there is a chapter entitled *Why Not Ask Them . . .?*[1] *According to Harré, the best social investigator is a listening one, someone who loads as little baggage of his own as possible on to the enquiry he is making. By seeing people in the natural setting of their everyday lives and building up biographical profiles based on their own memories and stories, I hoped to achieve some kind of an understanding of a culture very different to my own. I

*Notes and References begin on p. 174.

set out with the bare minimum of researcher's tools – a notepad and a pocket tape recorder.

Two years on from the *Bangkok Post* article I had spent over six months in Thailand, during which time I travelled extensively in the country. My research relied on observation and interviews with *kathoey* in Bangkok, Hua Hin (a town 300 km. south-west of Bangkok), Pattaya (a major tourist resort 150 km. south-east of Bangkok), Hat Yai (a town in the extreme south of the country, near the border with Malaysia) and the island called Ko Samui. Only two of the people I asked declined to be interviewed. The others agreed for the price of a drink or a meal, or simply because they liked to talk about themselves. These interviews were conducted mainly in English, my command of Thai at this stage being no more than rudimentary. There was no fixed place where the interviews took place. This, I felt, was probably as close as it was possible for a researcher in the field to get to the lives of these folk. Nevertheless all the time I was interviewing or note-taking I could not totally shake off the image of me and them – my inevitable position as 'outsider', myself as the *farang*[2] interviewer, my interviewees as the subjects or objects of the enquiry. Although there was no *a priori* reason to distrust what people said, indeed they gave every appearance of speaking openly and honestly, how could one be absolutely sure that their stories were 'pure' and not dressed up or processed in some way for their Western inquisitor?

Back in England I determined to learn to speak and understand the Thai language more thoroughly. So when I returned to Thailand for my third extended stay I was able to carry out a conversation in Thai and, most of the time, understand what was being said and make myself understood. The time and effort I had spent learning the language led to an important break: a Thai family invited me to stay for as long as I liked at the family home. The daughter was *kathoey* (Akorn, in the childhood narrative, but Daeng as she was later to become) whom I had met at one of the cabarets in the town. It was the combination of three things – a mutual enthusiasm for theatre and dance, Daeng's naturally outgoing and effusive character and my ability by now to speak passable Thai – that led to this unsolicited invitation which I duly took up.

The other ingredient required to take advantage of this serendipitous opportunity was a great deal of time. This I had and so I stayed with the family for nearly two months, hardly seeing or talking to another *farang* during this time. For some curious reason not mixing with other *farang* was a kind of unspoken precondition of being accepted into the household, which consisted of Father, Mother, Grandmother, Daeng and *mae barn*, the housemaid. It was a large house by Thai standards, located in a well-to-do suburb of Chiang Mai, and in addition to the immediate family there was a constant throughflow of 'uncles', 'aunts' and 'cousins'. I use quotes because in Thailand these terms are universally applied somewhat loosely and often refer to close friends who are neither blood relations nor in-laws. Daeng had many friends, most of whom were *kathoey*, among them Malee. Two other *kathoey* lived in the house on a semi-permanent basis and others were regular visitors.

A purist might argue that the very presence of an outsider in these circumstances would alter the daily rituals and flow of activity and might even encourage distorted – for example, exaggerated – accounts and stories. But the life of the household gave every appearance of carrying on as normal. Father was a semi-retired architect and expert on ancient buildings in that part of south-east Asia. Mother taught courses on northern Thai cuisine and was about to open a bakery from her home, and Grandmother helped *mae barn* with household chores and the rest of the time watched TV. Moreover, being a full-time member of the household, it was often possible for me discreetly to validate the accounts of individuals' lives that were to unfold by confirming these with other members of the family and friends.

I was welcomed into the house with traditional Thai hospitality, sitting down to share in what looked like a banquet. This turned out to be nothing special at the house since most nights friends of the Father, mainly professional people and civil servants, would join the dinner table and enjoy the cuisine for which Mother had justifiably gained a wide reputation. For the next months I was to enjoy Thai cooking, the like of which I've never tasted before or since. I was shown my room. In it was a small desk that had been cleared of everything so that I could use it as a work place. My only sacrifice was a certain loss of personal liberty in the clear implication that as part of the household I would be expected to share meals with the family and generally participate in family life. It was also expected that when I was not working I would accompany Daeng as companion/teacher and help her improve her fairly basic English. This was the deal. And of course I got to practise my Thai full time. Daeng at this time was performing in two shows every evening at different venues in the town, so my evenings, as well as my days, were fully subscribed.

In the months that followed the pocket tape recorder I had brought with me sat on the desk, unused. I had a unique opportunity to enter a community that was effectively otherwise closed to *farang* and also as much time as I liked. I therefore decided from the outset to desist from asking direct questions, at least for the time being, and let stories unfold over the dinner table, in the park, at the bar, on the coach, in the dressing room . . . wherever, naturally and in their own time.

As the weeks went by genuine friendships developed with the members of Daeng's family and with many of those who formed the exotic troupe of performers, with whom I was to spend so much time. I knew it would take time for confidences to be gained and for a level of acceptance by this community to be reached that transcended the status of *farang*. But I had the time and the language, and would eventually get to this 'privileged' position, as one of the professors in the Department of Sociology and Anthropology at Chiang Mai University was later to describe it. It was in a minibus hurtling from one theatre to the next, crammed with costumes, headgear, props and a dozen *kathoey* when I cracked a bad-taste joke in Thai, which was received with much amusement, that I knew I had 'arrived', so to speak. Thereafter I became privy to a dozen confidences, concerns and pleas for advice. One minor criticism of *kathoey* by the general Thai community is that they talk too much (*phoot mark, mark*). I was soon to find there was some truth in this. My painstaking deliberations about details of research methodology began to appear somewhat quaint against the sometimes overwhelming outpourings of these people. I learned more about *kathoey* during these weeks than I had throughout the preceding two years' research.

As it turned out, the desk that the family had so thoughtfully prepared for me was barely used. As soon as I closed the door and sat down Grandmother would appear with a coffee and a stream of northern Thai dialect, little of which I was able to understand. Then Daeng would appear and look over my shoulder asking me to pronounce this word or that and explain its meaning. Then I would hear my name shouted as a meal was being prepared.

Before going to Thailand that year (2000/1), I had made contact by e-mail with professors at two universities – Thammasat in Bangkok and Chiang Mai – and appointments had been set up for me to visit their departments and talk to them about the subject of my research. I had already been to Chiang Mai University on two occasions and had met and talked to some of the professors in the Department of Sociology and Anthropology. I had been shown the various libraries and told that I was free to use them and the facilities of the department at any time. So after a few days in my new temporary home, when it became apparent that my small 'office' afforded no privacy, I announced I would be working part of the day at the university. This at first met with some resistance but I was not prepared to be under 'house arrest', as it were, so insisted that this was necessary to my work because there were libraries at the university that I needed to use (partly true) and that this is how things were going to be. Very soon a satisfactory routine was established whereby I would spend three days a week, sometimes four, at the university and return home in time for an amazing dinner, conversation with family and guests and after this the dance performances in the main town.

I must have sat through a hundred of these performances, though the director was continually changing them and

introducing new pieces. The venue for the evening's first performance was a small stage set in a large enclosed compound
in the bowels of the Night Bazaar. The time of the show,
which lasted just over an hour, was 8.30 p.m. Every night
three of us, Daeng, another dancer who lived at Daeng's
house and myself, would arrive at the dressing room on the
back of Daeng's motorcycle in time for costume fittings and
a brief from the director/choreographer as to the format of
the show which varied each night, but was the same at both
venues. After the show the performers posed for photographs
and tips from the punters. A core of the performers were paid
a modest salary of 2,000 baht a month (about £35) plus the
tips they were able to procure. A few were not paid at all and
depended entirely on tips. While the core performers were
under contract to perform two shows every night, the unpaid
dancers were not obliged to do so providing they gave the
director reasonable notice that they would not be turning up
so he could find stand-ins or vary the show accordingly.
However, most of the unpaid performers, including Daeng
and her friends, in spite of the unreliable tips they would
receive, would dance most nights. They enjoyed dancing and
a strong sense of theatrical camaraderie bound the performers together.

The second performance was in a semi open-air venue less
than a kilometre from the Night Bazaar. This started at about
11 p.m. The cast had the loading, stowing, transportation
and unloading of costumes, props and themselves down to a
fine art and we would arrive at the second venue around 10
p.m. with an hour to spare. This we would spend at one of
the bars close to the dressing room with two or three tables
pushed together so as to make room for everyone. For the
performers this was a precious time of day, totally dedicated
to gossip. Even when the show began, those not actually on
stage or doing a lightning costume change would urgently
return to the clutch of tables, not wanting to be left out of the
conversation, often back on stage only just in time, occasionally late, for their next cue. The covered stage, also used
for kick-boxing matches when ropes were rigged around its
perimeter, stood in the centre of a large open-air piazza

surrounded by bars and cafés. The whole setting was relatively informal and the sound system drowned out the by no
means muted exchanges between those dancers who were
not at that particular moment on stage.

The (mainly) good-humoured banter would continue for a
while after the show when the dancers had changed out of
their final costumes back into their everyday clothes. After
this some of us would repair to another bar or a live music
venue playing a mix of Thai and Western music where we
would sit and talk some more into the night. This happened
a lot and if the mood was right they would break into spontaneous dance much to the appreciation of the late-night
clientele.

With my research tools now paired down to a mere note-
book, in which I would make long entries every day, was this
to be the totality of my investigation? For someone looking
for a 'slice of life' insight into a community very different to
their own, nothing could be better than for a time to become
part of this life. But cabaret dancers represent only one
expression of *kathoey* culture in Thailand, albeit a high profile one. They are ubiquitous and are to be found in a wide
spectrum of professions. There are probably more in what
may loosely be described as 'arty' careers – costume design,
hairdressing, photography and the media – than in academia
or commerce, but a few have office and administrative jobs.

Surprisingly, the group with whom I mixed appeared
largely ignorant of the history of Thailand's *kathoey*.
Questioning them about this would elicit only the vaguest
kind of reply such as, 'There have always been us in
Thailand' and 'Many, many hundreds of years' . . . etc. True
there were indications of a long history of this subculture in
their rites-of-passage accounts, in the ubiquity of these
people throughout the country and the acceptance (though
not always approval) of them by normal gender Thais as part
of the furniture of the broader culture, and indeed in the very
presence and provenance of the term '*kathoey*' itself. But it
was clear that a proper understanding of this group would
require some historical quarrying. My task eventually had
become clear. It was to set down on paper a biographical

style narrative of those individuals who had by a stroke of luck become my friends and to present this in the context in which I found myself and against a back-cloth of Thai history, tradition and myth.

All the narrative passages in this book are faithful to the accounts of the individuals in question. I confess to allowing myself a small artistic licence in reconstructing the school years of the three main protagonists, and inventing dialogues, but the stories are theirs, as told to me by each one of them. The factual details are corroborated with the help of a senior teacher at the school and professors at Chiang Mai university. The descriptions of people and places are authentic but some of the locations and all the individuals' names have been changed for reasons of privacy. 'Interpretation' on my part has been kept to a bare minimum – apart, that is, for the theory of the role of *kathoey* in the religious order, given in Chapter 13, which is pure interpretation. The narratives concerned with issues of childhood rites-of-passage, and the subsequent ones tracking adult careers and various episodes in people's lives are true stories.

The general information and insights about *kathoey* written down in this book are primarily the result of conversational interviews with forty-three individuals over the course of three years, all of whom I met and spoke with more than once. Fifteen of these I got to know fairly well. Of these, five were to become long-term friends, among them the three whose biographies appear as part of the text of this book. Indeed it was only possible to sketch landmarks and key incidents in the lives of these three because they became (and continue to be) my friends and I had gained their confidence.

A note needs to be added concerning the meaning of the term *kathoey*. For reasons that I hope will be apparent from the text, there is no Western parallel to this and similar categories of people in other countries, such as the native American *berdache* and India's *hijra*. This means that there is no word in English that delivers an exact translation of these terms. Anthropologists have struggled to come up with a term that best describes these subcultures but is not demeaning or patronising in any way. These efforts have produced

some curious jargon, such as 'two spirit', or 'gender liminal'
persons. There are many institutions and traditions amongst
the countries of south-east Asia that are incommensurable
with those of the Western world, and *kathoey* represent one
of them. It is quite inappropriate to describe them using
Western terms such as 'cross-dresser', 'transvestite' or 'gay'.
Even the recently imported term 'ladyboy' lamentably
obscures the history of these people and their traditional
place in Thai culture. If to us they represent a weird class of
person, only dimly understood, to Thais they are and have
been for centuries a familiar part of everyday life. I have
therefore chosen where possible to keep the original untrans-
lated term, *kathoey* (roughly pronounced 'kateuyee') and to
refer to the more general class of which they are part as
'transgendered people', or, 'the third sex'.

Chapter 1
Rama V School

There is one thing about Rama V School, located in the out-skirts of the city of Chiang Mai, in northern Thailand, that is distinctly *unlike* any school in the West. Namely, of its 1,100 boy pupils, aged twelve to seventeen, some 5 per cent have decided that they want to become girls.[1]

The school itself is about as big as a secondary school gets. The building, once an abattoir, runs the entire length of a street. Leftovers of the past, ugly iron grills and barbed wire lattices, decorate the outside wall whose height completely masks the interior from passers by. But for the unmistakable sound of some 2,000 school kids going about their daily business the odd structure might well pass for a zoo or a vast aviary.

That year, 1989, almost exactly half the school consisted of boys, and the other half of girls and despite its stark aspect from the outside, inside it was a happy place, made up of a well planned layout of classrooms, refectories and play areas. When the day's teaching was over the sounds of ball games, orchestra practice and a dozen spontaneous outbursts of fun were blended and confused by the echoes from the high walls.

Apart from lessons about the Buddha, the teaching was not unlike that in a Western school. By 1980 the engine of globalisation was well revved up throughout south-east Asia and the world was beginning to demand of its aspiring nations similar orders of skills wherever you happened to live. Agriculture has historically been the backbone of the Thai economy and in the early 1980s Thailand had enjoyed a powerful period of growth, only to be dashed in 1997 with overstretched banks and a collapse of the currency.

The aspiring 5 per cent can never of course become

complete girls in an anatomical sense, but they can and do enter a significant subculture that is universally acknowledged but not publicly proclaimed. Thailand has many secrets from Westerners or *farang*, as we are known, and this is one of them. A persecuted minority? Certainly not at Rama V School. Here these people are bold and proud, prank players and cheer leaders. By their late teens they have a dress style and body language that is distinctive. To aspiring younger boys they represent heroes (or should one say heroines?) and role models. Their exceptional appearance – their naturally smooth faces, sleek figures and feminine features – marks them off from other children and is the foundation for becoming a unique and, to Western eyes, mysterious form of being: a *kathoey*.

What follows is Akorn's story of his momentous step towards becoming a *kathoey*.

Akorn's story

It is near the end of the last term of the school year and teaching for the day is over. A hot day. Akorn and Manat sit in the shade of a canopy to the side of the main play area. They are watching Lek, their friend, play volleyball. Lek is a good player and will one day captain the school team. Already, by the end of his second year, at thirteen he has been spotted by the games teacher. He is small for his age and will never be as tall as some of the older players, but he will more than compensate for this with sharpness and agility. Akorn and Manat look on admiringly.

Three very different children, both in appearance and interests. Lek, lithe-limbed, round-faced, black-eyed, alert, swerving through the players with the elegance of a raccoon flying through the tops of coconut trees. Lek the sportsman, the dancer, the fun-lover. Manat by contrast tall, almost gaunt, a face bewitching in its seriousness. Manat the lover of theatre and art, the pensive intellectual. Manat with the smile it was not possible to look away from. And Akorn, a child of average height, average intelligence and staggering beauty, with his wide eyes, quizzical face and silky hair.

Akorn, blessed and gifted by the Gods and Buddha. Almost everyone in the school played a musical instrument. Occasionally, when Akorn picked up his violin, listeners were transfixed by the beauty of his playing and improvisation.

What bound this unlikely trio of friends together was simple. They were the only three in their class of thirty-seven second years who knew they wanted to be *kathoey*. Manat and Lek had come to this realisation three years ago but Akorn knew when he was six years old. Or was it earlier? He couldn't remember. He could vaguely recall jealousies of the kindergarten girls, his dislike of his maleness and a desire to wear girls' clothes. In their frequent discussions of what it would be like to become *kathoey*, what it would involve, how they should proceed, how they would tell their parents, it was always Akorn in the lead, Akorn the one with the knowledge, the incisive vision, the clarity of purpose.

The term was drawing to a close and the three friends had made a plan. Or rather Akorn had made it and the others had agreed. He would speak to Saowanee. Saowanee was a *kathoey* in her final year. She had settled into the role gradually over a period of three years and had earned the universal respect of pupils and staff at the school. Respect for her looks, her musicality, her Geisha-like grace of movement, her dress style, make-up and a warm and agreeable nature. She had a place next year at Chiang Mai University to study dance and theatre and she was keen to audition for the highly regarded *kathoey* student dance troupe called 'Rosepaper', whose annual cabaret was hugely popular with the other undergraduates. It was performed first on the university campus to packed houses and wild applause. Then maybe the show would be booked for a three-month run at one of the big tourist hotels in the town.

Like *kathoey*, the tradition of Geisha dancing girls in Japan has a long history. Training of a Geisha is highly structured. It begins early in life and continues for more than a decade. It is mapped out in progressive stages of achievement, almost like exams, in musicality, dance, dress, grace of movement and etiquette. Each stage is entered into with a degree of formality, ritual and negotiation. Successful passage through it confers status on the young aspirant. Thailand, unlike Japan, does not work to such strict and formal rules. In this sense Thailand is almost the antithesis of Japan. Thailand's deep-rooted and universal commitment to '*sanuk*' – which roughly translated means 'fun' – gives rise to social orders that are more spontaneous and whose dynamic is more fluid and less predictable. Becoming a *kathoey* does not require the calculated precision of becoming a Geisha.[2]

There are, nevertheless, well worn paths and one of these is for the young aspirant to acquire an older 'sister'. In the case of Geisha this is an elaborate process taking place against a back-cloth of politics, negotiation and the handing over of money. In case of *kathoey* it is simply a matter of approaching an older person whom one admires and trusts and asking them for their help, patronage and guidance. Having a 'sister' is usually a one-to-one affair, but Akorn insisted to Lek and Manat that he would ask Saowanee to be a sister to them all. Each time they met up with Saowanee it would be the three of them all together. Term time was running out and Akorn wanted to put his request to Saowanee before the weekend, which meant tomorrow, Friday. He would wait until she was on her own and then make his approach. The others endorsed the plan and admired his daring.

The following day whenever he was not in lessons, Akorn sought out Saowanee, watching for an opportunity to catch her on her own. But every time he found her she was with a group of friends or chatting to one of the teachers. Lunch time came and went, and by the time lessons recommenced he realised he would have to wait until the day's teaching was over. If this meant missing his usual bus and lying to his parents, then so be it. He knew that Saowanee normally travelled to her home, an apartment located in the centre of the city (Saowanee's father was a lawyer, a member of the relatively new middle class), by *songthaew*, an open air taxi-truck, that arrived some thirty minutes after school had finished. He would say he had to go through some work with one of his teachers. He hid in one of the small music cubicles used for practice and guessed the time his bus, bound for the foothills to the north of the city via his home in the suburbs, would have arrived and departed, transporting with it the familiar crowd on their way home for the weekend. He wondered if the others would notice his absence.

Akorn crept out of his hiding place. The school was emptying fast and there was no sign of his usual bus companions. He searched around. Yes, there was Saowanee saying goodbye to some friends. She was fumbling in her bag. He heard her shout 'See you tomorrow' and then something about the university. His chance had come so he took it.

'Saowanee!'

Saowanee spun round.

'Akorn', She looked at her watch. 'Haven't you missed your bus?'

'Saowanee, please may I speak to you?' Uncool, but he couldn't think of any other words.

Saowanee gazed at the small figure hurriedly approaching. As she would recount later, she had a sudden flashback of her own past and she knew immediately what was coming. The courage it took. The sickening fear of rejection. The appalling possibility that the thing you worshipped might turn out cold, indifferent, mocking even.

'Yes Akorn, of course you can speak to me,' she said. 'Come on, walk with me to my taxi.'

Akorn, now flushed, broke into a run and drew alongside his idol. Saowanee seemed to take her time.

'Have you missed your bus just to speak to me?'

'Well . . . er . . . yes . . . I said to the others . . .'

Now Saowanee looked concerned.

'I said I'll talk to you, but please, no "others".'

'I'm sorry, I didn't mean . . .'

'Akorn, my taxi will be here in five minutes. Say what it is you want to say to me.'

Tears welled in Akorn's eyes.

'Saowanee, I want to be . . . I want to be like you. Will you be my sister?'

Out it came. It was not the first time Saowanee had been asked this question, as she later told Akorn. She recalled with a twinge of guilt the anxious, disappointed faces. She was in her final year, indeed her final fortnight of school. She had a place at Chiang Mai University. She had every ingredient for a bright future, so why, she thought, fog it with extra duties? Being an elder 'sister' is no light matter. It involves months, sometimes years, of help, advice and support. First of all you must prove to yourself that the expressed wish is real and not just a passing whim. Then, fresh styles, new clothes, shoes, make-up, hair, new name, and not least, oh no, by no means least . . . parents. She knew from the experiences of some of her contemporaries that this could be very tricky indeed. When and how to approach them, what kind of a reaction to expect from the father. Saowanee's own family had been sympathetic and supportive, but she had a friend, Ae, whose father beat her up so badly that she had been away from school for a fortnight and was now living with her grandmother. This kind of reaction can backfire on everyone involved.

However, there was no escaping the fact that Akorn seemed deadly serious. She knew it the moment she had seen the look on his delicate face as he made his determined approach. She saw that, like herself, this individual's destiny had revealed itself at an early age, five or six perhaps, and that there would be no going back. It was uncanny. She was looking at a reflection of herself, aged thirteen; herself with exactly the same clarity of vision and intent. Akorn was *nang-fa jamlaeng* sure enough – a 'transformed angel' or 'angel in disguise' – and the realisation came to Saowanee that despite her painstakingly defended freedom from obligations of this kind she could not deny this person. She decided to help him/her through the years that lay ahead. From that moment Akorn became her *norng-toey-nang-kor* – her 'beautiful younger brother'. The *songthaew* was approaching.

'I will be your sister.' She spoke the words slowly.

Akorn's heart missed a beat.

'And the others . . .?' he said.

'Others?'

'Lek and Manat, my two very best friends. I promised . . .'

'I will be *your* sister.' Saowanee repeated. 'No others.'

The vehicle had pulled up. Saowanee turned to Akorn with

a big smile, touching his arm. Then she swung herself on to the bench of the *songthaew* and waved goodbye to the figure standing alone and still in the late afternoon light. Akorn stared at the disappearing vehicle. In the last ten minutes he had become *norng-toey-nang-kor*. Maybe.

That night Akorn's elation gradually gave way to anxiety. He could not sleep. He had intended his request to be 'on behalf of' the three of them. He saw himself as the trio's appointed delegate and for some reason it hadn't occurred to him that Saowanee would accept him but not Lek and Manat. What was he to say to them at school on Monday? Whatever he said he knew it would be no good. Apart from their disappointment it would inevitably drive a wedge between him and his two closest friends.

By the time morning came it had become painfully clear to Akorn what must be done. Saowanee would either have to take on all three of them or none of them at all. Unfortunately the situation was unfair to everyone involved. Saowanee wanted her freedom to go on to the university with no residual commitments. She had shown kindness and understanding to Akorn. He could see that to load an extra burden of responsibility on her at this stage, in the forms of Lek and Manat, was unreasonable. On the other hand, there was no way he could wave goodbye to the others and say, I'm O.K. my friends, but sorry, you must look after yourselves. He should have thought this through more carefully from the start. Of course Saowanee would say no, she already had. All the hopes and aspirations of ten hours ago were now dispersed. He got out of bed and composed this letter.

Saowanee – Thank you so much for saying yes to be my sister. I know next term you go to university and want to be free with a fresh start. I am sorry I asked you and understand that this is difficult for you. That's why I was over the moon when you said yes to me. You are the most beautiful person I have ever seen in my life, but I did not think carefully before I came to you. You see, I promised my best friends Lek and Manat – we were all at primary school together – that I would ask you to be sister to all of us. Now I think that was very stupid of me and am so sorry. I realise it is not fair to you but thank you again anyway. I know you will have a great time at the university. Good luck and I hope maybe one day I will see you again later in our lives. I will think of you every day. Will you remember me when you are famous? Forever your admirer, Akorn.

At school on Monday morning he acted boldly. This time he was not going to hang around and wait for Saowanee to be alone. As soon as his bus arrived, before lessons began, he sought her out. She was with a group of friends. Akorn simply ran up to her, pressed the little note into her hand, and ran away. The group watched the vanishing boy in silent astonishment. The others turned to Saowanee full of questions, but Saowanee was inscrutable. She pocketed the note with a turn of the head that implied the matter was trivial and not available for comment.

Saowanee's story

Later that morning when she found a private moment she read Akorn's letter, silently cursing the scrap of paper on which it was written. She almost tore it up but did not. Distractedly she folded it and placed it in one of the pockets of her stylishly modified dark blue one-piece school suit. She switched her mind to other things. Tomorrow she would not be in school. Every year the university ran a two-day advance induction course for students-elect who lived in the Chiang Mai area and for any others who were prepared to make the journey from more distant parts. Saowanee had enrolled for this at the beginning of the school term. She had been looking forward to the university visit all term and intended to enjoy the two days on the campus. These second-year mosquitoes would just have to get on and do their own thing without her help. She told herself the unfortunate episode was over and forgotten.

Chapter 2
Chiang Mai University

Saowanee's story continued

Chiang Mai University (CMU) lies four kilometres to the north-west of the city centre and is overlooked by the dense tropical forest of the Doi Suthep range of hills. To Saowanee it seemed like a small town, its teaching faculties, dormitories and sports centres sprawling over 725 acres and separated by shaded walkways of large trees. When the plans for the university campus were drawn up a special effort was made to spare as much of the original forest as possible. A large lake, the Ang-Kaew Reservoir, to the north of the campus, serves as the water supply for the university. There are several residential 'villages' for staff, shops and banks, restaurants and even a night market.

On the morning of the first of the two induction days talks were given by academic and administrative staff. These were followed by lunch, and after lunch three films, each about 35 minutes, about the history of the place and how its various faculties had evolved over the years and the recreational and social amenities that were on offer for students to enjoy. After this there was half an hour of rather awkward mixing with staff and then everyone went home in eight taxi-buses commandeered by the university.

The second day was less formal. The 150 or so students-elect were split into groups of ten and each of these groups was assigned to a guide for the day. The guides were all third-year students who had volunteered for the job. Their brief was to familiarise their charges with the layout of the campus and its facilities and to answer any questions they may have. Apart from these requirements what they did with the rest of the day was up to the student guides. Lae, Saowanee's 'sister' for three years, was one of these guides and she had made sure that Saowanee was assigned to her group. Those school-leavers in Lae's group were the lucky ones because Lae had organised the briefest possible tour of the campus (it would take a good week to get used to, so this could wait until next term) after which they would cool off with a swim in the Olympic size pool. Lunch was provided in one of the canteens but Lae had asked her group of school-leavers to bring picnics. These they would take to the lake and enjoy under the shade of the palms to a chorus of cicadas which was, by some bizarre ancient instinct, alternately *pianissimo* and *fortissimo*.

Lunch was supplemented by a coconut and lemon drink, spiced with just a dash of Thai rum, that Lae had supplied and which was her invention. The post-lunch 'question-time' was conducted with everyone sprawled by the lakeside and soon degenerated into Lae's clever parodies of some of the teaching staff. This was hilarious but also shocking to the novices as in Thailand teachers are generally regarded with a reverence second only to that accorded to monks. But Lae's dead-pan delivery had them all rolling about, gasping for breath.

Come mid-afternoon Lae woke up those who had dozed off in preparation for the two last items in this increasingly deregulated induction. First a walk in the lower hills of Doi Suthep to the north-west of the campus where footpaths cut through the jungle. Saowanee became aware of a different quality of hooting bird call and a different timbre of cicada. Finally, another swim for anyone who wanted it before they boarded their buses bound for the final journey home.

Saowanee, however, did not board any bus. Lae had some further plans for her. Most of those studying at the university lived in one of the thirty or so dormitories scattered around the campus. Among these was a dormitory specifically for *kathoey*. It was on the balcony here that a student cabaret troupe, known as 'Rosepaper', were rehearsing their latest show which they would perform at the end of term to the other students. Saowanee looked at the rails of richly coloured costumes, head-dresses, fans made of huge feathers and shelves of make-up that littered the place, relishing the prospect of the next years here. Lae had invited her to sit in on that evening's rehearsal. She could even try on some costumes if she wished.

First they went together to a nearby eating place and enjoyed noodle soup, chicken and mushroom rice, spicy salad and Singha beer. Saowanee felt like an undergraduate already. Lae reckoned she would have no problem when she auditioned for Rosepaper next year.

Supper over, they began preparations for the rehearsal. A *kathoey* cabaret show, is above all, a visual spectacle. Appearance is everything and two hours were taken for making up and getting into the first costume. There were twenty-two performers and up to twelve costume changes in this show. This meant considerable preparation and concentration was intense on the faces that stared at themselves in mirrors. Each person would do her own make-up with occasionally some help from a friend. Saowanee was impressed by the precision of this art. She still had a lot to learn. She watched Lae apply foundation, colours, glitter and the delicate lines, pondering the commitment expected of an older 'sister'; the demands that she, Saowanee, had placed, and would surely continue to place, upon this person. She looked around the room. *Kathoey* like to gossip but it was deadly quiet now as paint and glitter met flesh. Only the susurration of textile on skin broke the silence as costumes were donned and fussed over.

The company had only two technicians, one for lighting and one for sound. There was no stage manager as such. Cueing was done by the cast members themselves. By the time the show reached its first performance in front of an audience it would be highly polished with timing and cues on auto-pilot. But this cabaret was more than just a show for the other students. After the end of term performances at the university theatre it would transfer to the prestigious Westin Plaza Hotel for a three-month run and possibly on from there to another big tourist hotel. Nat, the clever, slightly built, ambiguous law student, looked after the business side of things and made damn sure these opportunist establishments paid a half decent fee, not the paltry one with which they always opened negotiations. They may be students but the show is highly rated in Chiang Mai and most Rosepaper performers go on to have a professional career of some kind in dance.

Neither of the technicians was here for this rehearsal because there were no lights to operate and the sound could be roughed on a cassette tape operated by Nat. The final rehearsals would take place in the university theatre with full sound and lighting rigs and several technical run-throughts. These were not popular with the cast who had to perform piecemeal and wait for a lighting cue to be set or re-set. But everyone knew these runs were essential and they started and stopped when told to, noticeably without the zest and smiles vital to the end product.

Today's rehearsal was a straight run-through in full costume. They had already done four of these. But when there are some 150 costumes for the dancers to deal with, organisation is everything. Costumes had to be laid out in the right order on four long rails. If a fast change was required of someone, another off-stage performer would be assigned to help with this.

The entire performance was cued by a tape of traditional Thai, Chinese, Korean and Japanese music to which the performers would dance in a style and costume appropriate to that country, as well as Thai and Western songs when one of the dancers would mime the words. Without split-second timing the result would look shoddy and amateurish. But with timing spot on, every movement of mouth and face perfectly choreographed and synchronised, the illusion was complete and the result mesmeric. Behind all dance and ballet that appears natural and flowing lies a background of intense training and rehearsal.

Eventually, make-up and dress were done and the costumes placed in their correct order in the cramped rehearsal space. Everyone was silent and tense. Nat waited a short time for the adrenaline to flow and then started the tape. Saowanee looked on as frozen anticipation cracked into action. It was like an old-fashioned clockwork toy you wound up to full tension before releasing its catch.

Saowanee had seen *kathoey* on stage before. Most up-country villages had a *loi krathong* fair – a festival held in November on the night of the full moon. This marked the end of the wet season and the beginning of a stable period of good weather when the farms could hopefully look forward to a time of good returns from their labours. The festival was organised by a committee of monks from the local temple. In the large village that Saowanee's family liked to visit each year there was music, *ramwong* (a dance form) and *likay* (comic opera) and often a beauty contest involving a group of travelling *kathoey*. This was immensely popular and drew a large and boisterous crowd of spectators. The contestants would parade on a stage first in stylish dresses and then for the second round in swimsuits. This happened against a background of much wolf-whistling, drinking and covert betting. Women were not allowed to stay in the temple, but because they were classed as *phet thi-sam* – the third sex – that is where the visitors were sometimes accommodated for the night.

The show had started. Lae had bet Saowanee 100 baht that she, Saowanee, would not be able to spot Lae's first appearance. Saowanee had accepted, telling Lae she was crazy and that she counted this easy money. On to the makeshift stage sprang six long-legged, high-heeled, laughing creatures wearing glittering black, gold-spangled thongs, silver necklaces and tall yellow and green feather head-dresses. They danced to a modern Western tune.

Rosepaper was known for its talented performers and the energy and synchronism of movement was indeed impressive. The music was of Western origin but the extraordinary movements were distinctly un-Western. In a single expressive movement, arms would extend not in straight lines but in complex curves counterpointed by bird-like swoops of the hands and fingers – their origins in the ancient dances of India. Faces sparkled not with the saccharine smiles of a television variety show but with joy springing from the Great Source, the Buddha. The beauty contests Saowanee had witnessed with her family in the past seemed static and contrived. They were nothing compared with this. In this first, voiceless, exuberant sequence, here was *sanuk* – 'fun', 'happiness' laid out; life as it is idealised in Siam. So far, no sign of Lae.

The second number. A solo. It was Diana Ross in a floor-length turquoise dress, a silver spangled top and a delicate green floral hair decoration with long dangling silver earrings. She was lip-synching perfectly to a well known track, strutting confidently in character across the performance space mouthing into a dummy microphone. The dancer could just be Lae, but with the shaggy wig, the heavy make-up and the wild movements it was surprisingly hard to tell. But by the end of the piece Saowanee had decided it wasn't her.

Next came a group of eight dancers all dressed in traditional costumes made of rich brocades adorned with sparkling costume jewellery resembling the apparel of royalty and celestial beings as depicted in classic Thai mural paintings. Two of them were masked. Was one of them Lae? Again, it was not easy to tell. The dance/drama (the two are inseparable in classical Thai performance) was a variation on the *lakhon*, its plot drawn from a folk myth about a princess's love, betrayal and death. There were no words in the piece. The story was explained in stylised sequences of movements. The fingernails of five dancers were extended several inches so as to add expression to the complex fluid movements of the trunk and hands.[1] One dancer manipulated two large fans. This gentle piece was brought to a conclusion with each character gracefully bowing to an imaginary audience.

Then Wham! Thai rock – a furious hybrid of Western and Thai rhythms and melody. Six dancers in calf-length orange outfits with silver trimmings, silver necklaces, orange feather head-dresses and long black trailing sleeves. Six more hot on their heels with the same style costumes but in deep blue, silver and black. Now enter a tall figure – the Principal Dancer. It was Lae in absurdly high heels and a glittering floor-length black dress with silver and gold spangles, a simple silver necklace and head gear of gigantic black feathers enveloping her face. The precisely choreographed fiery movement was electric, the effect fantastic as the dancers now interwoven, now in separate circling groups, competed for the elusive black goddess who seemed to fly and dive through the blue and orange figures with their swirling black trailers.

Exhilaration and expectation gripped Saowanee. Next year she would be one of these swirling angels with their rainbow smiles. And she would go on. Oh yes, she would go on to the biggest and best theatres in the land; maybe to Calypso in Bangkok or Alcazar or Tiffany's in Pattaya, where they danced to packed houses of coached-in tourists and became national celebrities. This wonderful spinning dance was the world. For a while she let herself indulge these fantasies. But they became clouded with thoughts of Akorn and her own selfish dismissal of his earnest request.

The show paused and a hand on her shoulder broke Saowanee's trance.

'So, did you spot me?' Lae's voice asked.

'Of course, in the black feathers.'

'No, but before that?'

'Ah, one of the masked dancers?'

'Diana Ross,' laughed Lae, delighted. 'You owe me 100 baht.'

Saowanee tried to laugh back.

'What's the matter?' asked Lae.

'Oh, nothing really, just passing thoughts,' Saowanee smiled back.

But thoughts of Akorn would not go away, even when she left the university later that night and found an empty bus whose driver agreed to take her home. Lae had been a great 'sister' to her that day. What kind of a 'sister' would she, Saowanee, make? She thought about Akorn again and by the time the bus stopped at the door of her apartment she had worked out what she must do.

Chapter 3

Biological Accidents

What gives someone apparently born a boy such an intense desire to become a girl at such an early age? Are such people different in their biological make-up from most folk who are content with the gender they are ascribed when they are born? Are we to look for an explanation in the chemistry of the person's body or elsewhere, for example, in the families and upbringing of the person?

Biological Theories

During the early weeks of life in the womb the potential for the embryo to become male or female is there but the structures are virtually identical. That is, the tissues from which ovaries and the female sex organs, and testes and the male organs, will develop are yet to become differentiated.[1] Subsequently, due to the action first of sex chromosomes and, later, of hormones (oestrogen in the case of females, testosterone in the case of males), the sex organs, following normal development, start to take on their respective characteristics. Even in the fully developed foetus the resemblance of male parts and female parts to the original common structures is still apparent.[2]

At birth, in most cases, the biological sex of the baby appears obvious. But not invariably is this so. A few babies are born with ambiguous sex organs – both female and male parts. Medically speaking, in these cases the gonads contain both ovarian and testicular tissue and the person is described as a (true) hermaphrodite. Hermaphroditism is defined as 'a congenital condition of ambiguity of the reproductive structures so that the sex of the individual is not clearly defined as exclusively male or exclusively female'[3]. In Western countries

such cases are likely to be dealt with surgically, and prompt-
ly, so that the person can be assigned to one gender or the
other. This is considered desirable and fair in that it avoids
the social and legal complications that would arise if the sex
of the individual were to remain unclear.[4] Very different attitudes towards hermaphrodites prevail in less developed parts
of the world. In some cultures hermaphrodite babies are simply not tolerated and are killed at birth. In others, the
Navaho Indians being one such example, hermaphrodites are
highly valued people who are considered to possess special
spiritual powers.[5]

Instances of true hermaphroditism, that is physiological
ambiguity, are comparatively rare. The great majority of
Thailand's *kathoey* are transgendered males, or 'pseudo hermaphrodites'. In my own study of forty-three *kathoey* none
claimed to be a true hermaphrodite. The ages at which the
decision was taken to be like girls varied from age three to
the mid teens, but the great majority knew this is what they
wanted by the time they had reached puberty. Only three had
undergone full sex reassignment surgery, twenty-one had
breast implants and thirty-nine were or had been receiving
hormone supplements. All forty-three had enjoyed, or were
presently enjoying, relationships with men and only one
reported a previous relationship with a woman.

First and foremost, these are people who have at an early
age rejected the ways of a boy in favour of those of a girl.
They express a strong desire to dress like women, to act like
women and to take on women's work – in short to be in
every respect like women. The same is true of many other
transgendered communities throughout and beyond Asia, all
of whom are recognised within their culture as being of a
gender of their own with its own particular culturally embed-
ded descriptive label.[6]

Normally, transgendered males will exhibit a preference
for a male partner. However, the anthropologist, Sabine
Lang, in her essay, 'There is More Than Just Women and
Men,'[7] spells out an important point: the concept of males
living like women (and vice-versa), that is embodied in the
special words that cultures have to refer to these people, is

not to be conflated with the concept of sexual preference, or homosexuality. She observes, for example, in a north American Indian transgendered subculture, originally called the *berdache*, that it is not unusual for transgendered males to have relationships with women and transgendered women with men. She uses the term 'woman-man' to refer to a trans-gendered male and man-woman for a transgendered female.

> The earliest sign that a person will turn out to be a woman-man or a man-woman is not an interest in sexual relationships with members of the same sex, but a marked interest in work activities belonging to the role of the 'other' sex. This will be noticed by other members of the individual's community, and it will result in a reclassifica-tion of that individual in terms of gender.[8]

Lang stresses that such people are 'reclassified' not on the basis of simple bipolar gender reversal – male to female, female to male – but, like *kathoey*, they are seen as a distinct third gender.

These observations would seem to imply that, in any dis-cussion of *kathoey* or other non-normative groups, the bio-logical make-up of the individual, the gender of that individual and the sexual preference of the individual must be treated as three separate, albeit interrelated, areas. The construction of gender in societies that recognise and define these groups is not commensurable with that of the Judaeo-Christian world. Their concepts and categories cannot there-fore simply be collapsed for the sake of convenience so as to concur with the traditional Western bipolar distinction male-female, man-woman, and heterosexual-homosexual.

Chromosomes

Chromosomes contain the genetic material, the DNA (deoxyribonucleic acid), that is the code of life. A normal person, whether male or female, has a total of 46 chromo-somes each made up of large numbers of genes. Of these 46 chromosomes, 44 are grouped in 22 pairs. These are known as autosomes and they determine the characteristics of an individual but not his or her sex. The normal male has 2 additional sex-determining chromosomes, known as X and Y, and the normal female also has 2 additional, known as X and X. A normal male therefore has a total of 46 chromosomes and his genetic make-up, or karyotype, is expressed as 46,XY. A normal female also has 46 and a karyotype 46,XX.

Mistakes and accidents are not uncommon in nature and this is true of the processes by which a person acquires his or her genetic make-up. Such mistakes can result in abnormalities in the individual's genetic constitution, some of which (mutations) are replicated and passed on down the genetic line, i.e. inherited, others of which are congenital, i.e. present from birth but not inherited or subsequently passed on.

Congenital Errors

The potential for congenital errors in the sexual development of a person is there from the very beginning, from the moment of fertilisation of the egg at conception. It arises again at critical points in the development of the embryo in the womb, and again during the biological transformations that take place during puberty.

In the early stages of the embryo's career in the uterus, the cells that will eventually determine the sex of the baby are indistinguishable. By seven weeks some differentiation is apparent but most of the structures are still 'neutral', in the sense that the existing clusters of cells still represent potential organs of either gender. It is at this point when the action of the X or the Y sex chromosome really starts to kick in. The genetic code of the X chromosome contains instructions for the male traces to be dismantled and for the as yet undifferentiated cells to become ovaries rather than testes and eggs rather than sperm. The genetic code of the Y chromosome issues the opposite command, resulting in the development of testes. When they are formed the testes will produce male hormones which stimulate the growth of male genitalia and effectively eradicate the female structures. But if the instructions coming from the Y chromosome are unclear, or ineffectual, female organs develop and the embryo becomes (in external form, at least) female. Androgen Insensitivity Syndrome (or Testicular Feminisation Syndrome) describes one such condition in which the baby is born with the outward appearance of a girl but is found to have the chromosomal make-up of a male and male levels of circulating testosterone.[9]

Conversely, by misdirection, or interruption, of the genetic signalling, it is possible for a chromosomally baby girl (46, XX) to be born without ovaries, or with testes instead of ovaries.

One of the most important functions of chromosomes is to produce enzymes and hormones that act on the developing embryo. 5 alpha-reductase Deficiency Syndrome describes a different interruption to normal development that can occur in XY individuals. In this case, the Y chromosome is successful in its function of stimulating the growth of testes, but the testes make only some of the hormones needed for male development. In the absence of the important hormone DHT (dihydrotestosterone), male genitals cannot develop and genitals become female or ambiguous. The only partially successful action of the Y chromosome in these cases means that the person also cannot develop Fallopian tubes or a womb.[10]

Klinefelter's Syndrome

Klinefelter's Syndrome (KS),[11] first described by the American Harry Klinefelter in 1942, is a congenital disorder that affects boys and men. When the male sperm fuses with the female egg, the foetal cells have at least one extra X chromosome. The most common result is the karyotype 47,XXY – i.e. 44 autosomes plus three rather than two sex chromosomes. Because this condition is congenital and not hereditary, the parents of a KS boy do not have to worry about its possible transmission to their grandchildren, nor need they be more anxious than anyone else about having another KS boy.

A further variant of this condition is known as mosaicism, in which some of the cells in the body are normal 46, XY and others are 47,XXY. This is expressed as 46,XY/47,XXY. The majority of 47,XXY individuals are sterile and unable themselves to produce children, but some whose bodies include 46,XY cells are able to produce sperm and have children.

Estimates of the incidence of KS in live male births vary from 1 in 1,000 (0.1 per cent) to 1 in 400 (0.25 per cent) making it one of the most common congenital abnormalities.[12] Boys with KS have a normal male body shape, except that they may develop breasts during adolescence. Research on the characteristics of KS people does not yield any very clear conclusions. Some impairment in mental functioning has been reported in some of these individuals – learning difficulties, difficulties in concentration, difficulties with language and difficulties in socialising with other children. However, reports of these problems, their seriousness and their commonality are vague and often uncorroborated. KS boys are not routinely reckoned to need special help and most of them appear to lead more or less normal school and adult lives. Levels of the male hormone testosterone are reported to be normal up to puberty but thereafter may fail to rise into the standard adult range. These cases are associated with certain female characteristics such as low facial hair, reduced muscle development and fatty hip deposits.

Increased vulnerability to a number of physical and immune-system related disorders have been reported. These include increased risk of osteoporosis (brittle bones), and asthma. But again, much of the evidence is no more than suggestive, except for the incidence of breast cancer which is 20 times more common in KS individuals than in the normal male population (nearly 1 per cent of all breast cancers occur in men).

No medical intervention is routinely prescribed or recommended for people with KS. A supplement of testosterone may be suggested in instances where, for example, female, or non-male, physical features are a source of embarrassment, or to counter fatigue. However, the very long-term administration of testosterone, or indeed of any hormone, is not considered wise because of the known risk of side effects.

A parallel condition to KS, known as Turner Syndrome,[13] can occur in girls. This is the result of the subtraction, rather than the addition, of a chromosome to give the karotype 45,X in some or all of the cells of the body. Like KS individuals, most people with Turner Syndrome lead normal lives but are likely to be infertile. The incidence of Turner Syndrome among women is estimated at approximately 1 in 2,000; considerably less than the incidence of Klinefelter's Syndrome in men. It may be significant that this statistic broadly parallels the greater incidence of gender dysphoria amongst men than amongst women.

The external genitalia a baby is born with are of course its most obviously visible biological insignia. But, as we see from these special cases where something has gone wrong with the application of the genetic code, they are not the only ones. There are other, hidden factors describing the sex or gender of the individual, such as the genetic parameters of the cells of the body and the individual's hormonal make-up, and these do not always concur with the more obvious signs. Reliable statistics of the frequency of these conditions are hard to come by, either because the conditions themselves are not immediately obvious, or because surgery is hastily performed to assign the baby to one or other sex, and the whole business kept under wraps.

The purpose of this reference to biological gender ambiguity and its associated syndromes as these have been described in the medical literature is not so much to suggest that *kathoey* are necessarily the products of congenital accidents, or even to propose that KS is a condition widespread amongst *kathoey* or other transgendered subgroups. This remains an open question. The point is to illustrate that definitions of male and female sex, like those of masculine and feminine gender, are less clear-cut than is often assumed. School biology texts state the case in black and white; female is defined by XX and male by XY chromosomes. But these by no means give the complete picture. American anthropologist Ann Bolin writes:

Paradoxically, the more scientific the methods used to assess the biological sex of an individual the more cloudy the assessment actually becomes, as witnessed by the Olympic games discourses on evaluating the 'true' sex of an athlete.[14]

It may or may not turn out to be the case that there is a more than average number of KS cases among *kathoey* than among normal gender Thais. The limited research to date has all been carried out on Western samples, and this has not so far produced any evidence of a higher than average incidence of chromosomal abnormality in transgendered males.

The Brain

Nevertheless, it is a common and insistent lament of *kathoey* and of transgendered groups in other countries that they feel like women trapped in men's bodies. How could the psychological and physical expressions of the person be so mismatched? While much of the workings of the brain remain a mystery, we do know that it is the centre of consciousness, emotion and feelings. It would therefore seem logical to look for a structure in the brain that could be responsible for a person's gender identity. A plausible biological explanation for a strong transgender impulse to express itself in a young boy would be that the part of the brain responsible for gender identification, should such a thing exist, had developed along different lines in embryos which were to become transgendered males than in those which would turn into boys who did not suffer this painful gender dysphoria. The 'high risk' place and time for errors to occur would again seem to be in the womb at the critical stages when hormones exert their influence on the embryo's development.

In 1995 a team of scientists from the Netherlands Institute for Brain Research in Amsterdam published a research report in the prestigious scientific journal *Nature* that claimed to have found evidence that the brains of transsexuals are different from those of normal men.[15] They made a detailed post-mortem study of the brains of six lifetime transsexuals, in particular of a part of the brain, the hypothalamus, that is known from previous research to be a control centre for sex drive, sexual activity and the emotions. Comparing the brains of the transsexual sample, not all of whom were homosexual, to the brains of both heterosexual and homosexual men and to those of heterosexual women, they found that a part of the hypothalamus in the transsexuals' brains was more like that of women than that of either heterosexual or homosexual men. Moreover, no differences were apparent between heterosexual or homosexual men. In other words, this difference was specifically correlated with gender preference, independently of a person's sexual orientation. The data for this study were collected over eleven years and involved detailed neuroanatomical comparisons of the brains of six transsexuals, six heterosexual men, six homosexual men and six women. The structure within the hypothalamus in which significant differences were found is known as the central subdivision of the bed nucleus of the stria terminalis (BSTc), an area of the forebrain that is essential for sexual behaviour. This structure is normally considerably larger in men than in women, but the BSTc of those in the transgender sample was clearly more like those of women than those of men. The authors confidently conclude: 'Our study is the first to show a female brain structure in genetically male transsexuals and supports the hypothesis that gender identity develops as a result of an interaction between the developing brain and sex hormones.'

This study has had its critics. First the sample size was small, altogether twenty-four brains were looked at under the microscope, among them the brains of six transsexuals. However, the differences discovered were clear-cut and statistically highly significant. The size of the BSTc in the transgendered group was slightly (though not significantly) smaller than that of the women, so in this sense it could be said that the transgenders exhibited more extreme female patterns than the women in the sample. A more serious criticism was that all the transgendered group had been taking the female hormone oestrogen. The smaller BSTc in this group may have been the result of regular doses of this hormone, i.e. the indirect consequence of wanting to become a women rather than its cause. The authors cite additional detailed data from the study which they claim show that 'The size of the BSTc was not influenced by sex hormones in adulthood'. So the debate goes on. Certainly this study on its own cannot be held up as definitive evidence for the biological basis of transgenderism with its congenital origins in the womb. The business of changing gender and all the procedures and social difficulties that go with it cannot be without stress, and this itself could have had an effect on the brains of these people. However, as a preliminary study, it is intriguing and suggestive.

Other Physical Differences

Are there any other signs that transgendered people are different physically from people who are comfortable with their biologically given sex (that is, apart from any changes they have deliberately chosen themselves)?

Richard Green, professor of psychiatry at Imperial College, London, also appears to favour a congenital explanation of why transsexuals are as they are. In an address to the Royal College of Psychiatrists in the year 2000, Professor Green reported the results of a four-year study involving much larger numbers of people. Altogether 400 male and 100 female transsexuals were studied at the gender identity clinic at Charing Cross Hospital, London.[16]

This study found that more of the transsexual group were left-handed than were right-handed, completely bucking the trend in the normal population, the overwhelming majority of whom are right-handed. It also found that transsexuals' fingerprints tend to be strongly ridged. Both of these characteristics are determined in the womb, so here is further tenuous evidence for the congenital hypothesis. It is worth adding that all three doctors I interviewed in sex reassignment clinics in Bangkok had reached a conclusion, through their own experience and their interpretation of the research that has been done, that the condition of *kathoey* is present at birth and therefore a consequence of events in the womb.

Tallness

Another oblique but intriguing clue can be drawn from some not so scientific observations by myself and from the comments of some other authors. It does not take a statistical survey to reveal that on average *kathoey* are taller than other Thai males and females. And this is not just the performers. Everyone I spoke to in Thailand acknowledges this fact but no one seems able to offer an explanation.

When Spanish explorers first came to what is now southern USA, they discovered men living like women. Among the earliest of chroniclers of these times was one, Cabeza de Vaca, who makes the following comments based on his observations in the early 1500s.

> I saw a devilry which is a man married to another man, and those are some effeminate and important men. They go dressed like women, and they do women's work . . . And they are larger than other men, and taller.[17]

The information sheet on Klinefelder's Syndrome, prepared by Steve Hammet for KS organisations in the UK, and based on information from an impeccable list of academic sources states, 'Men with KS are usually sterile. They tend to have longer arms and legs and to be taller than their peers.'[18]

Roz Mortimer, producer and director of the film company Wonderdog Productions is currently involved in making a twenty-five minute film, intended for broadcast, with the provisional title *Gender Trouble*. The film's principal objective is: 'To challenge the current notion of sex being exclusively binary (male or female) and that intersex is an abnormality that requires a cure.'[19] 'Intersex' is the descriptive label used to describe people born with physically ambiguous genitalia (roughly equivalent to the old term 'hermaphrodite'). In a personal communication, I asked her whether, from her years of research with such people, she considered there to be any other obvious physical characteristics of these people and she referred to a tendency for them to be taller and to have longer legs. She raised the possibility that this may be due to hormone treatments acting to reverse a normal growth limiting process.

During interviews I conducted with three specialists in transgender surgery at Bangkok clinics, as part of my own research, above average tallness (compared to the general adult male population) was also mentioned as 'characteristic of about 65 per cent of *kathoey*'. But these doctors did not think this could be put down to the taking of hormone substitutes which they reckoned, if anything, would tend to inhibit growth rather than encourage it.

Upbringing

There is no question of Thai families calculatedly encouraging boys to act and dress like girls. Traditional Thailand is very much a patriarchal society that sets men superior to women, both socially and spiritually. But striking is the fact that many boys proclaim they want to be like girls at a very early age. Jeremy Marre's film, *Lady Boys*, made for BBC Channel 4 in 1992,[20] is a documentary about the careers of two northern *kathoey* teenagers. One scene revealingly shows one of the boys giving a kind of lesson or demonstration to much younger children. This is described in the film as a 'safe house for young *kathoey*' and it highlights the openness of *kathoey* culture in some parts of Thailand. *Kathoey* are ubiquitous and are an overt, not an underground, part of society. They are there for everyone to see and are clearly perceived by some younger boys as objects of fascination and even role models.

This observation is simple but important in an understanding of how such a subculture arises and continues to exist. The widespread presence of potential role models in the form of transgendered males, many of whom are held to be more beautiful than women (a commonly heard comment), can be seen as a necessary, though not a sufficient, condition for the existence of this category. There is clearly no equivalent in Western countries.

From the data I collected in my interviews, no evidence emerged of a higher than normal incidence of family problems. Five of the sample reported that their fathers had

disappeared or died when they were young.[21] This is probably a higher than average number, but could be due to a variety of factors specific to this particular sample. In any case,
most individuals reported a financially insecure but otherwise normal family life.

Conclusion

Good scientific research on the physiological make-up and
possible biological causes of transgender desires is itself at no
more than an embryonic stage. Nevertheless, research,
observation and debate does demonstrate that the biological
basis of a person's gender is by no means as clear-cut as traditional educational models have conditioned us into assuming. What few scientific studies of the physiological make-up
of transgendered people there currently are do not support
any very firm conclusions. However, they are consistent with
the opinion of medical practitioners working in this area that
a person is born a *kathoey* and that, at least in some cases,
this may be the result of events that occur in the womb.

Chapter 4
Saowanee's Plan

Saowanee's story continued

Saowanee's plan for Akorn and his two friends Lek and Manat had crystallised on the late bus back from the university to central Chiang Mai. It was a Wednesday night and she was not required to return to the school until the following week. But Saowanee had resolved not to wait until next Monday to put her proposal. Their meeting would require privacy and this was not easy to achieve within the precincts of the school. She would summon the three of them this Saturday and talk to them at her home where she would make sure they were not disturbed.

Saowanee relied on a word-of-mouth method of communication that is ancient to south-east Asia and a continual source of bafflement to foreigners. By these devices it was determined that the three boys would come to Saowanee's apartment at 10 a.m. on Saturday morning. Her plan set, Saowanee was taking a certain mischievous pleasure in the suspense which she knew this arrangement would cause. She was becoming aware that the occasion had some dramatic potential. Saowanee, very much the senior, the mentor, was for the first time in her life wielding serious power. Rather than see them in her bedroom she would arrange for her mother to show them into the study downstairs (her father was away in Bangkok on a court case). She would be 'out' but in fact would wait upstairs in her room for, what? ten minutes, maybe fifteen. She was discovering that the role of elder 'sister' had some mileage in it after all.

Lek and Manat had arranged to stay at Akorn's house on Friday night and take the bus to the city centre in the morning. They slept little and imagined a hundred possible scenarios for their encounter with Saowanee. Saturday morning came and their curiosity was intense. Why were they being summoned to her house and what did it mean?

A hotel worker having a smoke outside his back door looked on with curiosity as a battered red bus spat out three odd-looking kids near the main entrance to the temple at 7.40 a.m. on a Saturday morning. Most children their age would be helping their families on the farm or at home. There was certainly something strange about this trio. But the breath he drew to ask their business was cut short by the sound of his own name and a stentorian command for him to return to his duties.

For two hours and twenty minutes the three wandered the streets of Chiang Mai, heads buzzing with anticipation and lack of sleep. At exactly 10, Akorn, their natural spokesman, rang the electric doorbell. The door was answered by a calculatedly austere woman. Saowanee had involved her mother – from whom she had inherited her own acting talent – in the plot to intimidate the boys and the three were shown into the study where they waited for a lip-biting fifteen minutes.

Saowanee, dressed in a simple but expensive one piece knee-length dark green dress, composed herself in an upstairs room. She had decided that she was going to enjoy this. It was tradition for an older 'sister' to give her protégé, or in this case protégés, a rites-of-passage style hard time at their initiation and she would not shirk this duty.

She descended, entered the study, quietly closing the door behind her, and signalled to the figures standing awkwardly at the other end of the room to sit on the floor. This they did in the traditional style, feet pointing away from their senior. She drew up a chair and sat facing them.

'Have you any idea why I have asked you to come to see me today?'

A cruel opener which she almost regretted. Silence: the only possible response.

'OK. I'll tell you straight out. As you probably know I've spent some time at the university. During this time I've given some thought to the unexpected request that you, or rather Akorn on your behalf, sprang on me last week.'

Silence, still, from the floor.

'I wonder whether any of you realise the extent of the

responsibilities of an older "sister".' she continued. 'Quite apart from the obvious matters of teaching you dress sense, make-up and personal style, there is first of all the issue of your families. Have any of you broached the idea to your parents that you *may*, and please note I say *may*, want to change and become girls?'

'I think my mother has an idea,' Akorn said.

'An *idea*! Exactly what do you mean, an *idea*?' Saowanee was getting into gear.

'One day she caught me experimenting with my sister's make-up.'

'Oh yes – and what did she say?'

'She didn't say anything,' Akorn said.

'And you think that constitutes the promise of acceptance on her part?'

'Well, she didn't tell me off.'

'My dear child' Now Saowanee was really in her stride 'the absence of disapproval means NOTHING.'

Manat coughed in embarrassment. This was awful. He wanted to leave the room.

'Let me tell you now,' Saowanee continued. 'Breaking this kind of news to parents is extremely tricky. It can even be dangerous. I was lucky. My parents are loving and intelligent. They want for me only what I want and if my father felt any disappointment in me he didn't show it. But it's not always like this, believe me. Mothers generally are not a problem, but fathers can be. I know a family with a son about your age. Last summer he went to stay with his aunt and uncle in Laos. He returned home made-up and dressed like a girl. His father went bananas and I won't tell you what he did. And this sort of thing is not so uncommon.'

Manat whitened. They all sat motionless.

'Next question,' Saowanee went on. 'And I hope you can make a better stab at it than the last one. How old were you when you first conceived the idea of being like a girl rather than a boy. Manat, you first.'

'I was ten. I remember it quite well. That's when I had my first thoughts about it,' Manat replied.

'And you Lek?'

'About the same. Me and Manat were in the same class at primary school and we used to talk about it all the time, and sometimes sneak into Manat's sister's room and have a go with her make-up and try on some of her clothes.'

'And you Akorn?'

'Ever since I was born.' Akorn reconsidered his reply: 'At least as far back as I can remember.'[1]

Saowanee stared at this precocious boy.

'I put it to the three of you in all seriousness that you are still too young to reach a decision such as this which will affect the whole of your lives. You are flirting with an idea you only dimly understand. Maybe you do want a different way of life, but maybe at the moment this is just a childish fancy, a kind of infatuation, that could blow away like pollen in the wind. You see the change you are considering means closing off many options that our society offers a man – and these are plentiful and varied. My advice to you is to go away and think about it for another year, and if you're still serious we can talk again then.'

Much of this was standard openers and Akorn knew it.

'What age were you Saowanee when you finally decided to change?' he ventured.

'I didn't invite you here to discuss myself,' Saowanee attempted to reply.

'No but it is reasonable to ask you, isn't it?' Akorn insisted.

'No, it is not reasonable. It's bloody impertinent', Saowanee was struggling. 'All right. I was about the same age as you. But that doesn't mean anything. Everyone's different.'

'You know Noi?' Akorn asked. Noi was a *kathoey* in her penultimate year at the school.

'Of course I know Noi.'

'You know Noi runs a "safe house" for very young *kathoey* in her village?'

A 'safe house' consists of regular question-and-answer support sessions and basic instruction in dress and make-up.

'Yes, I know.'

'Well some of these kids are seriously young. The youngest

is about four or five. You disapprove?'

Saowanee knew this to be the case and had indeed herself been present at some of these meetings. 'No, I don't disapprove.'

'Well then.'

Game One to Akorn.

Saowanee got up, opened the door and shouted to the maid to bring them water. She switched on the fan. The sun's strength was starting to build to its fierce mid-day climax.

'Look, I'm not unsympathetic to what you want to do, obviously, or I wouldn't have asked you here. But you need to have some idea of the voyage you set out on and the rocks and tides that will alter your progress and at times make you want to turn back. The point is there *is* no turning back. Once you've decided to change from being a boy to being a girl you've left the shore. You turn your back on many, many places you could go in life in favour of comparatively few. There are a lot of *kathoey* in Thailand, but we are still very much a minority. We are recognised and acknowledged as a group of people. In some places we are admired on account of our talent. In some places we are not admired, just tolerated, maybe even ignored. Many people set out on this journey with enthusiasm only to find themselves alienated from their families, frustrated and without money. And what happens to them? Often they become prostitutes. Do you know in Bangkok there is an area where *kathoey* hang out to service the likes of taxi-drivers?'

'No way,' Lek interjected. 'I would rather die.'

'I'm doing no more than giving you some hard facts', Saowanee said.

'There are loads of *kathoey* in good jobs having a good time,' said Lek.

'Who do you know and in what jobs?'

'There's the cashier in Thai Farmer's Bank, the head chef at Chiang Mai Orchid, there's waitresses all over, there's the dancers, the photographic studios in Central – oh, come on, they're everywhere. And, yeah, there's the volley-ball team, half of whom are *kathoey* and they're doing really well in the National League.'

'You're into sport, aren't you Lek?' Saowanee commented.

'He is, he's captain of the juniors at school. He's seriously good,' Manat interjected.

'He is so,' Akorn said.

The maid entered the room with glasses of cold water for everyone.

'What about your bodies?' Saowanee said, bluntly. Everyone except Akorn blushed.

'It's easy for me,' Akorn replied. 'I want to be just like a woman. I want breasts and I want to start the hormone treatment as soon as possible. Then I want implants because someone told me that you shouldn't go on hormones for too long. So I'll go on hormones until I have enough money to pay for implants. They say collagen is better than silicone . . .'

'You think you know it all', Saowanee fumed. 'You know nothing. And what about your penis. Will you cut that off with a pair of scissors, or what? Here, there's a pair on the desk, so why don't you do it now?'

Saowanee was flustered. Akorn was not.

'I don't like my penis. I've never liked it and in due course, when I can afford it, I shall have the surgery. Will you have it?'

Saowanee gazed at the extraordinary child. No question about this one. She turned to the others.

'How about you Manat?' Manat was speechless.

'And you Lek?'

'I think I want to keep an open mind about any surgery,' Lek said. 'I think I will take the hormones, like Akorn, but I'm not sure about implants or surgery.'

'Manat?'

'I would never have surgery. I don't really like the idea of any unnatural alterations to my body. But I do know I want to be like a girl and dress like a girl and live like a girl and have a boyfriend.'

Saowanee felt her role as Grand Inquisitor starting to dissolve. She was putting them through the test and she was impressed. Lek and Manat were staring at the floor. Lek was flushed and there were tears in Manat's eyes. Akorn looked her in the eye.

'OK. So what about names. Have you thought about your new names?'

'We talk about it all the time,' Manat said.

'Akorn?'

'My new name will be Champagne.'

Saowanee's jaw fell open.

'Lek?'

'I want to keep my name because it's OK for a girl.'

'Manat?'

'I would like my new name to be Saowanee,' he stuttered, 'If that's OK with you.'

'Yes, It's OK with me Manat.'

Saowanee took a long drink of water. 'I'm prepared to offer you all some help.'

The atmosphere was cut by a knife.

'Now I cannot on my own be "sister" to all three of you. This would be just too much for a single person and it would not work out. Just think about it and you'll understand. Yes?'

Three heads nodded expectantly.

'Here's what I propose. I go to the university next term as you know. You will be starting your third year at the school. I will agree to be Akorn's sister and also to help you, Lek and Manat, as a kind of half-sister. Do you know Som at the school?'

They nodded.

'Som and Noi will be in their final year at the school next year. Som will be your "sister", Lek, and Noi yours, Manat. I'll oversee things and be, well, more like an aunt than a half-sister, I suppose, as the senior with two assistants. All six of us will keep good contact, working kind of as a team. This way responsibility can be shared and it shouldn't be too much for any one person. How does this sound?'

'It's brilliant,' Lek said, 'But have you spoken to Som and Noi yet?'

'I went to see them yesterday, and they're both more than happy with the plan and said they think it would be fun. They're both good people, and well worth nailing before someone else does. I've provisionally arranged for us all to meet up next weekend. I'll buy you all colas at Central and we can start getting down to business.'

Their ordeal over, and her plan accepted by the others with much gratitude and enthusiasm, Saowanee told them about Rosepaper and the cabaret at Chiang Mai University. She described the costumes, the dance forms, ancient and contemporary, and the professionalism of the much practised cues and changes. She planned to take the three to see the show when it transferred to the Westin Hotel, after the end of term. She would be able to get complementary tickets from Lae. She knew the excitement this would generate, so she would save this particular item of news for their next meeting.

The three went back to their respective homes in muted and conspiratorial mode. They had been accepted into the sisterhood, which is the first stage of becoming *kathoey*. They were under instruction to say nothing at all to their parents until this had been thoroughly discussed over the course of their next meetings. Their new careers had begun and they were comfortable in their awareness that now there would be no looking back.

Chapter 5
Buddhism and a Third Sex

About 95 per cent of Thais are Buddhists. Buddhist monks are to be seen everywhere throughout the country and are unmistakable with their shaved heads and saffron robes. The life of a monk centres round one of the 30,000 or so temples or *wats* where the monks live their frugal and abstemious lives. Many Thai men (indeed *most* Thai men until comparatively recently), including the king, spend some time during their life serving as monks in a temple – anything from a few days to several months. It will be obvious to a visitor that Buddhism is more than just a notional religion. It has been the cornerstone of Thai society since it was embraced as the country's official religion in the thirteenth century AD. However, Buddhism first arrived in Thailand from India and Ceylon long before this, probably around the third century BC.

Animism
Before this time Animism, or spirit worship, had been the core 'religion', not only in Siam, as Thailand used to be known, but throughout all south-east Asia and beyond. Indeed, it is probably fair to say that some form of Animism predated the arrival of more formal, scripture-based religions in most parts of the world, although its expression in the particular rituals practised were very much a provenance of the local culture. The essence of this most ancient of belief systems is the notion that spirits reside in and control all things natural and supernatural.

Beliefs in spirits (*phii*) persist in Thailand to this day. The beneficent spirits of the hills, forests and waters are celebrated in festivals and worshipped through the ritual markings of respect and by the giving of gifts. Demonic and mischievous spirits, often attributed to the misfortunes or misdeeds of people's ancestors, are the ones responsible for all the ills of the world, and these must be propitiated and repelled by offerings, sacrifices and symbolic tokens.

Anthropologists have described festivals and rituals in the remoter north and north-eastern parts of the country, where industrial influences have yet to penetrate, that one can imagine have changed little over the course of 2,000 years or more. Mary Mills[1] describes a widespread panic in the villages of north-east Thailand in 1990 when the villagers believed they were under attack from an army of dangerous widow ghosts (*phii mae mai*). They defended against this by such means as parading phallic symbols through the villages, painting their nails and cross-dressing. Echoes of old Animist traditions linger on in rituals such as these which are, even to this day, common in the remoter parts of the country. Not just in these rural areas but throughout the whole of Thailand little 'spirit houses' are to be seen, supplied with an image of the Buddha, sacred symbols such as elephants, charms and offerings and often small bowls of rice, milk or other food. These serve two purposes. They represent a containment, or 'home', for the spirits of the land and space on which a nearby house, or maybe a hotel, has been built. And at the same time they constitute a shrine at which prayers and offerings can be made to the Holy One.

In their dual role these spirit houses are monuments to the peaceful fusion of the old Animist beliefs and traditions with the newer Buddhist ones. The two appear to stand quite comfortably together. Whenever Christian invaders of a country encountered Animist practices it was a very different story. Their only recourse was to a rhetoric of 'devilry', and 'vileness' and all too frequently a policy of suppression and persecution. One seventeenth-century Christian's perplexity at the apparently harmonious coexistence of priestly (Buddhist) practices and Animist ones in Siam is nicely illustrated in this extract from a journal of a Director of the East India Company written in 1636:

However these Heathen be thus religious, yet they fear and serve (although contrary to the opinion of most of their Priests) the very Devils, whom they believe to be the authors and causes of all evil. They adore these unclean spirits in their sickness and misfortunes, celebrating their feasts with instrument playing and offering atoning sacrifices of fruits and living creatures. They are so strangely abominable in their gestures and actions, that it is not fit for a Christian either to see or write them.[2]

The old Animist practices did not pose the same threat to the Buddhists as it did to the Christians. The adoption of the doctrine of Buddhism in thirteenth-century Siam did not involve overturning and replacing Animist beliefs but rather embracing and incorporating them. The ancient superstitions about spirits and the mischief they can potentially make live on in the spirit houses, the wearing of amulets, the 'exclusion zones' monks make by surrounding a newly built or newly blessed house with long lengths of holy string, using holy water and lengthy chants to expel and contain these bearers of bad luck.

A similar process of integration happened when Hindu Brahmanism arrived, also from India, in the eleventh century AD. Religious life in Thailand over the past 1,000 years has been a mixture of these different influences, which were eventually to shake down into modern-day Buddhism, with echoes of the past in the representations of Hindu gods in the temples and the Animist superstition and magic that is deeply entrenched in the everyday life of all but the most cosmopolitan communities. The story line in many contemporary feature films and television dramas made in Thailand incorporates a ghost, or spirit, of some kind, signalling misfortune. In the Buddhist system these are spirits of people that have died in unfortunate circumstances and have yet to be reborn. The spirit is temporarily homeless, free floating and potentially dangerous. Most malevolent of all is a *phii graseu*, believed to be the spirit of a woman who died during pregnancy and represented by the lurid image of a disembodied head attached to a trail of intestines.

Buddha

The Lord Buddha, or Enlightened One, Siddharta Gautama, was born an Indian prince in about 500 BC. In his mid-life (scholars disagree over his precise age), he renounced his material wealth and devoted his life to developing a doctrine based on Hindu beliefs that was to evolve into the Buddhism of today. The founding principle of this doctrine is that the life of a human being is embued with suffering in the form of a struggle against carnal desires and material greed. The ultimate goal of a person's life is to strive against these forces through a regime of asceticism and self-denial. Life is, in this sense, represented as a tension between the human drives with which a person is endowed and an idealised state of purity which he must struggle to attain. The person, or his or her inner soul, is subject to an indefinite number of reincarnations – re-births – in different forms. He gains *kamma*, a kind of metaphysical credit, through the worthiness and self-lessness of his deeds and the serenity of his everyday demeanour. Conversely he loses it, or gains *negative kamma*, through yielding to and indulging carnal cravings and worldly living.

Kamma is therefore a kind of spiritual bank account with entries representing credits and debits. There are many ways of gaining credit and avoiding debt and these are laid down in the forty-five volumes of *The Tipitaka*, the basic scriptural canon of Buddhism. The most effective way of gaining credit is by becoming a monk. If sufficient kammic credit is accumulated through the person's life or lives, that person attains the ultimate state of *nibbana* – literally the extinction of suffering – so that reincarnations cease and they become one with nature and the spiritual dimension and achieve the state of Enlightenment.

The concepts of *kamma* and reincarnation are of Hindu origin (Hindu *karma* and *nirvana*),[3] and were reinterpreted by the Buddha in a fresh, dynamic way that clearly appealed to people on account of the optimistic potential of the core message: it is possible for anyone to achieve Enlightenment as a direct consequence of their own actions. And, moreover, it can be achieved in this lifetime, or if not, there were limitless 'second chances' in lives to come. Buddhism in various forms, springing from different interpretations of the original writings, was to spread in due course to Sri Lanka, China, Nepal, Tibet, Central Asia and Japan.

It is widely believed that the teachings of the Buddha were not written down until the second half of the first century BC. The contents of the *Tipitaka* were initially passed on by the Buddha's disciples as oral traditions and then transcribed at a later date in Pali, a dialect of the Sanskrit language. The Buddha apparently preferred the more popular vernacular of Pali to the formal language of Sanskrit used by India's priests and intelligencia. Later the Pali canon was translated into Sanskrit and large tracts of the Sanskrit version were subsequently translated into Chinese and Tibetan.

Male, Female and . . .

The *Tipitaka*, in contrast to the Christian Old Testament, identifies not two gender types, male and female, but four. The four genders are male, female, *ubhatobyanjanaka* and *pandaka*.

The Pali Text Society's *Pali-English Dictionary* defines *ubhatobyanjanaka* as 'Having the characteristics of both sexes, hermaphrodite'.[4] Khamhuno, a columnist on Buddhist weekly affairs, defines them in Thai as '*kathoey thea*' or 'true *kathoey*', that is, hermaphrodites.[5] But Bunmi Methnkum, Buddhist scholar and head of the traditionalist Abhidamma Foundation, finds references to two types of *ubhatobyanjanaka*, female and male. A *purisa-ubhatobyanjanaka* is someone who is born male but when attracted to another male loses his masculinity and takes on the mental attitudes and physical features of a female so that he/she is able to have heterosexual relations with this man. An *itthi-ubhatobyanjanaka* is the gender opposite of this, i.e. a woman attracted to another woman who gains the characteristics of a male.[6]

Definitions of *pandaka* are equally diverse. 'A eunuch, weakling' (*Pali-English Dictionary*), 'A *kathoey*, a castrated man or eunuch' (Thai translation of the *Vinaya* – a portion of the *Tipitaka* concerned with the rules of conduct for monks),[7] 'A person who has a deficiency in the signs of masculinity (for men) or femininity (for women)' (Bunmi),[8] and 'a person who takes pleasure in having relations with a man while feeling that they are like a woman' (Thai language summary of the *Tipitaka* by Suchip Punyanuphap).[9] This last definition equates *pandaka* with *kathoey*.

Although it was never colonised, Siam and its border states, like most countries throughout the world, has seen its share of internal conflicts, changing principalities and redrawn boundaries over the centuries. All the north was once the kingdom of Lanna (the million rice fields), with its own ruler. Lanna endured longer than the two other principalities, Sukothai and Ayutthaya, only losing its semi-independent status in 1939 when it came under the direct rule of Bangkok. The different kingdoms, each with its own geographical and political boundaries, naturally gave rise to different forms of Buddhism throughout the country. The tradition that prevailed in Lanna and the north is the relatively conservative *Therevada* Buddhism which remains Thailand's official religion to this day.

Below is a translation of an antique Buddhist palm-leaf manuscript, which is a portion of the northern Thai account of the creation of the world. Its translator, Anatole-Roger Peltier believes it to be based on an ancient oral tradition. This document also makes reference to more than two sexes.

When the world was not yet in existence, there were only the cold and the hot. By coming together and by 'feeding each other', these two states of matter gave rise to a wind that blew very strongly and called into existence the earth and water. The moisture released by rocks produced mosses and seaweeds which, in turn, gave rise to grasses, plants and trees. Insects such as fleas and beetles were born from the elements earth, water, fire, then beings endowed with bones and blood. From the element earth a woman called Nang Itthang Gaiya Sangkasi was born. The scent of flowers was her only food. Mixing her sweat with clay, she moulded animals so that they ate the plants that grew in plenty. From the element fire, a man called Pu Sangaiya Sangkasi was born. As he was out for a walk, he met Nang Itthang Gaiya Sankasi and the two of them became husband and wife. The couple shaped the first three human beings: a man, a woman and a hermaphrodite . . .

. . . the three human beings grew up and had three children. Itthi, the woman, showed great affection for Pullinga, the man, much more so for him than Napumsaka, the hermaphrodite. When he saw that the two beings loved each other tenderly, Napumsaka, the hermaphrodite, killed the man. The woman was grief stricken. She laid her husband's body in one place, planted a Jhalatun tree to indicate the place of the cemetery and offered food daily until the corpse had completely decayed. Shortly after that, the hermaphrodite died also. The woman put his body in one place and never came near it again, but went on offering rice to her deceased husband. The three children seeing their mother act this way, asked her: 'O Mother, why do you bring food to Father who died first, and not to Father who died last?' The mother answered: 'The first was dear to my heart and I loved him very much; as for the second, he was not dear to my heart and I had no affection for him'. Shortly after that, the woman died. The three children gathered the bodies of their three parents, staked out the cemetery and offered food every day without fail.

After their parents' deaths, the three children had thirteen offspring: six girls and seven boys . . . afterwards Itthi, the children's mother, reaching the end of her life, died. Pullinga, the husband, carried his spouse's body to the cemetery, staked out the site by planting a Thong Puang tree and offered food daily. Shortly after, Napumsaka, the hermaphrodite, died in turn. Pullinga placed his body in some place and cared no more about it. The children asked their father: O Father, to Mother who died first, you offer food daily on her tomb. And for Mother who died last, you don't do anything. Why is it that you don't treat them equally?' The man answered: 'O my darling children, your mother, the one who died first,

was dear to my heart; as for the one who died last, she wasn't.'
(From Anatole-Roger Peltier (1991). *Pathamamulamuli: The Origin of the World in the Lanna tradition*. Chiang Mai, Thailand: Silkworm Books)

This somewhat confusing story, as well as the text of the Pali canon, is quite explicit in its references to a person who is neither male nor female but whose gender is properly located somewhere in between these poles. *Ubhatobyanjanaka* and *pandaka* are both terms that have been rendered as *kathoey* in Thai translations of the Pali canon. In the above passage, the unfortunate, unloved hermaphrodites might be bracketed as *kathoey* in modern parlance. Indeed the *Royal Institute Thai Language Dictionary* defines a *kathoey* as 'A person who has both male and female genitals; a person whose mind and behaviour are the opposite of their sex/gender'. Another well-known Thai dictionary, compiled by Manit Manitcharoen in 1983, defines *kathoey* as either a man or a woman. The latter also makes the point that '*kathoey*' and 'homosexual' are terms that have different meanings:

> Homosexuals or the sexually perverted (*wiparit thang phet*) are not *kathoey*. The characteristic of a *kathoey* is someone who cross-dresses (*lakka-phet*), a male who likes to act and dress like a woman and has a mind like a woman, or a female who likes to act and dress like a man and who has a mind like a man.[10]

Broadly speaking, the older dictionary definitions have tended to ground themselves in biological characteristics – the hermaphrodite who possesses both male and female, or ambiguous, sex organs – and newer definitions have emphasised the mental, or psychological, aspect – the female psyche trapped in a male body, or, less commonly, vice-versa. Western medical statistics show that true hermaphroditism, that is, physiological ambiguity, is rare and there is no evidence of any difference in occurrence between populations of different ethic origin. Neither is there any reason to believe this state has been more common in the past than it is today. A case can therefore be made that those translations of ancient texts and legends that incorporate the term 'hermaphrodite' – indeed the legends themselves – do not necessarily intend this term to be taken in its literal, medical sense, but are using it to refer to some middle ground between maleness and femaleness. If this is so, then the term *'kathoey'* sits quite comfortably as an interpretation of the legendary descriptions of these people. I have not heard any modern-day *kathoey* describe herself as a hermaphrodite. Self-attributions range along a continuum from *kathoey*, meaning someone said to be born a boy but believes himself to be psychologically, or has a strong wish to become, a girl – to straight *phuying*, or 'woman'.

These legends stand in sharp contrast to the Christian account of the Creation of the World given in the Old Testament. Here there are just two human protagonists, Adam and Eve. In Buddhist mythology a third category is present that is rendered not as a variant of either male or female but an independently existing gender. The concept of more than two genders would appear to have been inherent in Thai culture right through from ancient to modern times. It is encapsulated in the early twentieth-century colloquial expression for *kathoey* as *phet thi-sam* – the 'third sex'.[11]

Peter Jackson, Research Fellow at the Australian National University makes the interesting observation that the word *kathoey* may not have a Thai etymology. Jackson cites evidence that suggests that the term derives from an ancient Khmer verb which means 'to be other/different'. The modern Khmer term for the third sex category is *katoey*, spoken with an unaspirated second consonant. He adds a footnote that, because of the close political, cultural and economic links between Thailand and Cambodia in recent centuries, many medieval Khmer words have been 'borrowed' into Thai and 'reborrowed' back into modern Khmer at a later date. This therefore does not preclude a 'trading' of the term between the two countries.[12]

Whether or not the word originated in the Thai language,

it is clear that it did not originate in the Indian Sanskrit language or the related Pali. Jackson speculates that the term
kathoey or its ancestor term predates the Buddhist writing,
and that the sacred texts served to reinforce a concept that
was already at that time part of traditional Thai and Khmer
culture.

In modern Thailand *kathoey* represent a minority group
that is recognised as an indigenous subculture and is for the
most part tolerated by gender-normative Thais and by the
community of ordained Buddhist monks – the *sangha.*
Indeed, in the *Vinaya* – the section of the *Tipitaka* that deals
specifically with rules relating to the monastic order – cases
are described of ordained monks changing gender and taking
on the physical attributes of women. The Buddha's reaction
to these cases is reported to have been tolerant. Providing the
individuals in question had shown themselves worthy members of the monastic order by following its rules and pro-
scriptions their ordained status was to be respected and they
were given permission to go and live with an order of nuns
and follow the nuns' code of conduct. However, liberal rul-
ings such as this would not be possible for long, as the order
of Therevada nuns was to disappear in medieval India and
could not, according to scriptural law, be reconstituted in
Thailand. As part of his scholarly commentary on sections of
the *Tipitaka*, Bunmi[13] notes that Ananda, the Buddha's first
cousin and personal attendant, is reported to have been born
as a *kathoey* in many hundreds of previous lives. It must be
added that the Buddha's tolerant attitude was not for long to
be extended to *pandaka*. The reason for his ruling that *pandaka* presenting for ordination should not be admitted to the
holy order appears to have been the disruptive behaviour of
one such ordained *pandaka* monk who violated the clerical
vow of celibacy in a very public manner, thereby bringing
disrepute upon the order.

The Buddhist Account of Kathoey

Apart from these unambiguous scriptural references to a type
of person who does not fit the European-American stereotypic

categories 'man' or 'woman', a further strong, if not com-
pelling, indication that *kathoey* have long been an integral
part of Thai culture is found in the fact that within the traditional Buddhist system of beliefs is to be found an explanation
of how a person becomes *kathoey*. According to this, a person's becoming *kathoey* is predetermined from birth and is the
direct result of kammic debt accumulated through misdeeds
committed in a former life. A person is re-born *kathoey*
because in a previous life they performed actions that violate
sexual mores. Such misdeeds include adultery, being a female
prostitute, sexually abusing one's children or failing to fulfil
an expected role in the reproductive process, such as a man's
not caring for a woman who is pregnant by him.

Bunmi is quite clear on the point that there is no escaping
the kammic consequences of such misdeeds and no avoiding
the burden of suffering which they load on to the individual.
Thus, being born a *pandaka/kathoey* is inevitable and is no
more the person's 'fault', at least in the life into which they
are presently born, than being born physically deformed,
deaf or blind.

Nor do any further kammic consequences accrue from
desires and actions that arise out of the state of being a
kathoey. Homosexual activities are not considered sinful and
do not affect the individual's kammic account. It is even possible for those who become *kathoey* to achieve *nibbana* in
this life if they conscientiously apply themselves to prescribed
Buddhist principles for attaining spiritual liberation. Bunmi
writes:

> Changing one's sex is not sinful. Consequently the inten-
> tion to change one's sex cannot have any ill kammic con-
> sequences. But sexual misconduct is sinful and can lead to
> consequences in a subsequent birth.[14]

'Sexual misconduct' in this passage refers specifically to heterosexual acts that break cultural mores and taboos in
respect of family life and the birth and bringing up of children. Homosexual activities fall outside this bracket and are
therefore kammically neutral.

Prasok, another Buddhist writer, says that much of the kammic debt of *kathoey* has already been paid off in a previous life when they were reborn into hell and forced to endure the torment of being chased by wild beasts. Their only possible means of escape was if they climbed the tree of hell (*ton-gniw*) which had spikes in its trunk and branches that tore the victims as they climbed.[15] Both authors agree that *kathoey* should be treated with compassion on account of the suffering they have to endure. Moreover, Bunmi maintains that everyone in a previous life has violated a heterosexual taboo at some point. It therefore follows that everyone at some stage has been a *kathoey*:

> The very people who laugh at *kathoeys* were themselves once *kathoeys*. Absolutely everyone without exception has been a *kathoey* because we have gone through innumerable cycles of birth and death, and we don't know how many times we have been *kathoeys* in past lives and how many more times we will be *kathoeys* in the future.[16]

The generally accepting and tolerant attitude towards *kathoey* throughout Thailand can perhaps be interpreted in the light of this causal explanation of their situation that is the legacy of traditional Buddhist wisdom. It is the unavoidable destiny of these people to be what they are and this places them outside the arena of moral sanction. They are to be pitied, maybe, but not judged.

The outbreak of AIDS/HIV in Thailand in the 1980s, however, saw a splinter group of Buddhist writers dissent from this traditional tolerant position to argue the opposite: that homosexuality was responsible for the spread of the disease and that it represented a conscious violation of natural sexual practices and was therefore to be condemned and participant individuals to be blamed. This was part of a worldwide panic reaction to reports concerning the AIDS phenomenon at this time. Its counterpart, trumpeted by Christian extremists, ran: homosexuality is unnatural and sinful, and AIDS/HIV represents a divine judgement and retribution against its practitioners.

However, as Peter Jackson comments, the impact of this burst of homophobic rhetoric amongst some Buddhist writers turned out to be relatively small. It was undermined when the magnitude of heterosexual transmission of HIV in Thailand and the rest of the world was discovered in the 1990s. According to Jackson, the generally tolerant public attitudes towards *kathoey* were not affected by what came to be seen as something of a hysterical over-reaction.[17]

It is important to be clear that, although the terms 'homosexual' and '*kathoey*' are occasionally conflated in modern commentaries, they represent different concepts, historically and semantically. In traditional Buddhist texts as well as in modern Thai-speak, the word '*kathoey*' refers to a class of person who identifies as being of non-normative gender. The concept would seem to have roots, or at the very least strong parallels, in ancient myths of the *pandaka* hermaphrodite. The meaning of 'homosexual' is unconcerned with gender orientation and addresses a preference for same-sex activity in both men and women. The term 'gay' is a relative newcomer, finding its way into the Thai vocabulary in the 1970s along with the invasion of copious other Western influences at this time. A trendy contemporary Bangkok gay who identifies and dresses as a man would not care to be called a *kathoey*. The term has been usurped, somewhat arrogantly, by this *nouveau* community to carry a derogatory connotation. Certainly, among the *kathoey* who became my friends, there was a general disdain for gay bars and night-clubs. Each of the two subcultures, like the concepts themselves, has its own very different social derivation and historical provenance with the consequence that the appearances, lifestyles and outlook of each are not commensurate and they do not easily mix.

Conclusion

Buddhist scriptures repeatedly refer to more than two genders of human being in legends of the origin of the world and in ancient canonical writings. This stands in sharp contradistinction to the Christian version of the Creation involving two people, male and female, Adam and Eve. The explanation for why a person becomes a *kathoey*, in Buddhist teachings, is that this is a direct consequence of having violated social mores through committing promiscuous deeds in a previous life.

The term '*kathoey*' has no etymological relative in Buddhist texts nor, according to Thai historian Peter Jackson, in the Thai language itself. It most likely pre-dated both of these and there are hints it may be of Khmer origin representing a concept that was reinforced by, rather than originating from, its counterparts in Buddhist texts. Whether or not this is so there is evidence that the concept has ancient roots. Given this is the case, and that the concept has prevailed to the present day for more than 2,000 years, we might speculate that other similar groups exist in different parts of south-east Asia. We know that many migrations and many alterations to territorial boundaries occurred throughout this stretch of time. We can also roughly trace the spread of the Buddhist religion over this period. With so great a dissemination of populations and ideas, why should the concept of a third sex, or gender, be something unique to Thailand?

As we shall see, third-gender categories of people are identified in other countries in south-east Asia, in all probability also of ancient origin.

Chapter 6

The Kathoey of Modern Thailand and Old Siam

In what he claims to be the first history of Siam to be written in a European language, W.A.R. Wood, a British diplomat to Siam, writes that 'The principal difficulty which confronts the writer who tries to compile a history of Siam is the almost entire absence of reliable native chronicles.' There are two main reasons for this. There was no written language in Siam until the thirteenth century A.D. The little that is known of the country prior to this date is gleaned from legends and folk traditions, and from the journals of various Chinese travellers. Later, the official records and annals of the kings of Ayutthaya (the old capital of Siam) were all destroyed when the Burmese captured and sacked that city in 1767. There were attempts made subsequently to reconstruct the history of Ayutthaya and the result was the *P'ongrawadan*, published in 1863, and, according to Wood, containing large numbers of errors.

Wood's book, *A History of Siam*, was first published in 1926,[1] and in spite of the 'difficulties' he refers to, this is a remarkably comprehensive, erudite and well written work from a man who went to Siam at the age of eighteen in 1896 as a clerk, translator and general assistant in the consular office in Bangkok, married a Siamese woman, and ended up Consul, Registrar and Judge of the British Consular Court in Chiang Mai. In all, Wood spent sixty-nine years of his life in Siam, and the titles of his later books, *Land of Smiles*[2] and *Consul in Paradise*,[3] first published in Bangkok in the 1940s, leave little doubt as to his affection for that country.

If Wood is correct in saying that many aspects of Siamese history remain obscure, then the history of *kathoey*, that ubiquitous but enigmatic subculture, is that much more so. American anthropologist Gilbert Herdt makes the point that the study of ambiguous-gender people is intrinsically difficult because these minority groups are often hidden away within the broader community.[4] Their ambiguous, quasi-taboo status inclines them to shun public scrutiny. And if many stick together as a defence against the gaze of their own countrymen they are that much more shy of *farang* (European and American) researchers and journalists wanting to discover more about them. Another Asian transgendered minority group, the *hijras* of India, provide an extreme example of this isolationism. They live and move in groups of their own kind and the only times they make an appearance in the broader public domain is in their traditional employment as dancers and performers on auspicious occasions such as marriages and births.[5]

Kathoey are sometimes caricatured in contemporary Thai popular media as loud mouthed, rather uncouth and exhibitionist. On the face of it this clownish stereotype is a long way away from the impression of a shy, introverted group such as the *hijras*. However, it is important to bear in mind that it is only comparatively recently that *kathoey* have come under public and international scrutiny. This has to do with their emergent popularity as cabaret artists. The first of the so-called 'ladyboy' cabaret shows appeared in Pattaya in the late 1960s and 1970s when this coastal town was being developed for tourism. Its popularity and commercial success as an entertainment for the tourists saw this style of show spread to Bangkok and other towns on the tourist trail as the industry expanded over the next decades. The cabarets themselves perform to mixed international audiences and are a curious hotchpotch of traditional Thai dance, dances in Chinese, Korean and Japanese costumes, and burlesque. The comic sketches contain a strong element of self-parody.

Those parts of Bangkok and Pattaya where *kathoey* prostitutes line the streets at night looking for customers also, on the face of it, present a picture that might seem to contradict the image of them as an introverted minority. But this too is a recent development and has sprung up as a result of a cash-driven incentive to service a growing demand among visiting foreigners. Take away these roles, both of which have arisen over the past forty years as a direct result of the tourist boom, then *kathoey* appear more like their low-profile counterparts in other Asian and south-east Asian countries, assuming traditional roles and jobs within their communities and shy of scrutiny by outsiders. These are the folk that represent the more authentic cultural legacy rather than those who have jumped on the bandwagon to entertain tourists in one way or another with the sole aim of making money. The very roles of modern hooker and cabaret performer – highly scripted as they are – provide a camouflage behind which the true provenance and identity of the person can remain hidden.

Neither should it be thought that because many modern day *kathoey* mix with Westerners they are more accessible to the researcher than the more secretive transgender groups of other cultures. The *farang* who meets a *kathoey* for the first time and asks her about her life is very likely to be rewarded with a familiar standard pack of lies – 'father dead . . . mother ill . . . broken heart . . . no boyfriend . . . no money to pay for apartment' . . . etc. This is not talking to the person, it is tapping into a well polished script – another artificial device for the real person to hide behind. Only by spending considerable time getting to know individuals on a personal basis is it possible to get beyond the façade and discover the rituals, beliefs and emotions that are the essence of these people's lives. This method, if it can be called such, is the same as that of Serena Nanda on which her writing about India's *hijras* is based. She argues that it is the only possible way of reaching an understanding of such people.[6]

The existing literature concerned with *kathoey* is limited and patchy. Prior to the twentieth century, the only Thais able to read and write were monks and nobility. Earlier documents surviving in the temples are almost all concerned with interpretations of Buddhist scriptures, composition of herbal remedies, and records of the construction of buildings and the tools used by builders and craftsmen. Thai academic historians concur that *kathoey* have traditionally been involved in religious circles,[7] yet no authoritative account of their precise place and role within the monastic system exists. The reason for this is that they are, and have been in the past, paradoxically, both accepted and also regarded as something of a taboo subject within the Buddhist monastic order. Taboo subjects are not uncommon in Thailand. For example, everyone knows that the payment of 'tea money' (bribes) to the police is a widespread practice but officially such corruption does not exist and therefore no official records of these transactions exist. However, neither the lay people of Thailand, nor the priesthood, nor the few academics who have written on the subject dispute that *kathoey* have been part of Thai culture for centuries. Australian anthropologist Peter Jackson writes that 'A study of Thai terms for the transgender role, Buddhist legends and other cultural data suggests a long history for the *kathoey* role among the Thai people.'[8]

But their traditional place in religious and secular cultures on the face of it appears mysterious, even paradoxical. How can *kathoey* be involved with the monastic order and at the same time remain a taboo subject within this order? To date no substantial thesis on the essential traditional role of these people within the wider culture exists. But there are enough pieces of the jigsaw for an intriguing picture to emerge.

Notwithstanding the consensus among academics, and among Thais in general, that *kathoey* have ancient origins, what actual evidence is there for this? In setting out to investigate the murky history of these people, a sound first step might be to try provide an answer to the sceptic who asks, 'consensus is one thing but what is there to prove that *kathoey* are no more than "ladyboys" – an opportunistic product of the booming tourist industry of the past forty years?'[9]

Siam

The first European nation to send an envoy to the Siam court was Portugal in 1516. The first serious interest shown by other European nations was in the empire-building years of the seventeenth century. Some journals of members of the expeditionary voyagers of this time have survived. These are mainly the records of envoys from nations whose purpose it was to establish trade links and diplomatic relations with Siam. One such is from the pen of Joult Schouten, director of the Dutch East India Company in 1636, who wrote, that 'They clothe themselves (both men and women) thin . . . both sexes wear painted petticoats'.[10]

Comments about the similarity in clothes and indeed in the roles of men and women are frequent entries in the journals of the early European visitors to Siam. Their authors were encountering what was to them an unfamiliar lack of demarcation between the sexes. Nineteenth-century British diarists, Sir John Bowring[11] and Herbert Warrington Smyth, also made the same observation. Smyth, for example, wrote:

> In this country [Siam], where the respective spheres of action of the two sexes are so little differentiated, where women smoke cheroots and men guide the plough, and where both are dressed alike, boy nurses have charge of the small children as frequently as girls . . . they seem singularly apt and gentle at the business, and handle their charge with a sang-froid which I must admit evoked my greatest admiration.[12]

Entries such as these show that their writers are picking up on a departure from the gender boundaries with which they themselves are familiar. There are no direct references in the sixteenth- and seventeenth-century European diaries specifically to a third or ambiguous gender. There is mention of concubines and eunuchs as part of the entourage of the king's court, but in neither case do descriptions of these people correspond even remotely to that of *kathoey*. Concubines and second wives were women, and eunuchs, castrated men, whose function it was to act as intermediaries between purveyors of food and goods and the women of the court.

Most of the attempts of the seventeenth century to establish diplomatic and trade links failed, and another recurring theme in the journals of the time was the frustration felt by delegates that the king seemed more interested in receiving gifts than in talking business. Nonetheless, nearly a century after the Portuguese, the Dutch established a presence in Siam in 1605, followed by the English in 1612, the Danes in 1621 and the French in 1662. These powers were not to coexist in Siam harmoniously. There was constant rivalry and jostling for position. By the 1680s the French had gained the upper hand with the help of a small army. In 1687 hostilities came to a head between King Narai of Siam and the British East India Company. By the end of this decade the king decided he had had enough of the infighting among *farangs* in his country and forcibly expelled the French garrison. The Siamese impatience with and mistrust of *farangs* had become deep seated and was to persist for a very long time. Siam virtually sealed itself off from the West for the next 150 years.

Not until the first half of the nineteenth century did Siam open its doors again to the West. The more visionary, less isolationist kings of this time could see the economic advantages of opening up their country, this time to a new class of Westerner – less the dignitary, more the professional. Into the country came consuls, lawyers, diplomatic staff, clerical staff, translators, surveyors and the like, some to spend most of their working life there. In addition, a new wave of missionaries arrived. The Catholics and Jesuits of the seventeenth century had long since been expelled. This time it was the turn of pioneering Christians from America who were to establish the first of the new mission stations as well as the first printing press.[13]

The delegates of the seventeenth century had been kings, princes, heads of state, noblemen and high-ranking officials. The Siam they saw and wrote about was the extravagant milieu of the king's court with all its pomp and ceremony, banquets, entertainment and the ritual exchange of fabulous gifts, such as elephants and horses. Their concern was the negotiation of territory and trade tariffs. The individuals this brought them into contact with were more or less exclusively people of a similar high rank to themselves. *Kathoey*, assuming they were part of the culture at this time, would have been a very humble part of it. According to Buddhist teachings they are damaged people, made to suffer punishment in the present life on account of sins committed in a previous one. They are not to be scorned because they cannot help being what they are in this life. If anything they are to be pitied. With such a balefully low status in the social fabric it is unlikely they would have been brought into contact with the educated dignitaries who were the visitors and recorders of this time. So perhaps it is not so surprising to find no reference to them in the journals of these early state expeditions to the country. The limited exposure of these travellers to the populace and the fact that the men and women of seventeenth-century Siam wore similar clothes and were of similar appearance would make any individuals of ambiguous gender extremely difficult for an outsider to identify.[14]

The new influx of Western immigrants and visitors in the nineteenth century, many of whom were to take up professional positions and set up residence in the country, were exposed to a much more diverse range of native people. If *kathoey* have indeed enjoyed a long standing indigenous presence in the culture it is more likely that some mention of them is to be found in the writings of the nineteenth- and early twentieth-century settlers than in those of the seventeenth-century European dignitaries who moved amongst royalty.

Sure enough, references to a class of people it is possible to identify as *kathoey* exist in these journals; again, not in the journals of state visitors who were the guests of provincial governors and the like and who were cosseted by police escorts, but in those of the foreign visitors who had dealings with the ordinary folk.

In his second book, *Land of Smiles*,[15] W.A.R. Wood reflects on his career in Thailand which began in 1896 as general factotum and ended as British Consul and Judge in Chiang Mai. He observes:

In Siam, especially in the north, there are a certain number of men who habitually wear female clothing and grow their hair long. It does not seem to be thought that there is anything morally wrong about this, and so far as I have been able to make out, these *Pu-Mias* (men-women), as they are called, really possess, as a rule, no moral eccentricities. Physically also, I am told, there is nothing unusual about them. They prefer to dress as women and that is all there is to say about it.

He goes on to describe one such case:

There used to be a young fellow of good family living near us at Lampang who sometimes dressed as a man and sometimes as a woman, and it was generally believed that during the first half of each month he actually was a male, and during the latter half of the month became a female. I often exchanged greeting with him (or her) and found her (or him) very pleasant and polite; but I never got on sufficiently familiar terms to justify me in making personal enquiries as to his (or her) sex. So far as I could make out, he seemed to be a young man of very attractive appearance, though a trifle girlish looking. He did not wear his hair long, but when sporting feminine costume was very fond of decorating his head with flowers.

The liberal Wood contrasts the accepting attitude amongst Thais of this gender fluidity with the rigid gender definitions in the England of the time (the 1930s) that could lead to criminal prosecution for anyone who departed from the male/female stereotype.

I read some time ago of an English *Pu-Mia* being chased across Hampstead Heath by an angry crowd, hauled up before a Beak, severely lectured on the hideous depravity of his conduct and heavily fined. Here, thought I, is one of the things they do better in Siam. Why bother about *Pu-Mias?* So far as I can see they do no harm, and in Siam, where nobody bothers about them or interferes with them, there is certainly little of the sort of thing which their existence, in the English theory, might be taken to indicate.

The following comment on the apparently higher incidence of male to female transformation than female to male
concurs with those of other authors. 'Female *Pu-Mias*, who
dress and behave as men, are not so common as the male
kind. I have only met one of them.'

An earlier reference to the presence of a transgendered
minority apparently integrated into the community is to be
found in the journal of H.S. Hallett published in 1890.[16]
Hallett was a surveyor and Fellow of the Royal Geographical
Society with specialist expertise in the planning and construction of railways. He had been sent from England with a
brief to carry out a feasibility study of connecting India (then
in British hands) with Burma, Siam and China by railway 'at
a reasonable expense and to select the best route, financially
and commercially for the undertaking'. The motive behind
the plan was to open up markets between the various countries, and via India, to Europe. The railway was never built,
of course, but from the tone of his narrative, Hallett appears
completely confident that this huge project would not present any special problems!

His journal is entitled *A Thousand Miles on an Elephant
in the Shan States* and it is a diary of a year's travels in 1877
through Burma and what is now northern Thailand. On their
arrival at the city of Zimme (now Chiang Mai) Hallett was
the guest of pioneering American missionary, Dr McGilvary
and his wife. During this break from what must have been
extremely arduous travelling by present-day standards
Hallett enjoyed a very hospitable few days' rest and recuper-
ation at the mission house and was able to explore the city of
Zimme at leisure. His diary includes this entry:

Following the road through the western suburb, I entered
one of the shops to purchase some Chinese umbrellas, as
mine were the worse for wear, and was served by a person
dressed in ordinary female costume, who seemed to be
very masculine in appearance, and considerably above 4
feet 10 inches in height – a height few Zimme Shan women
attain to. On telling Dr. McGilvary, he informed me that
the individual was an hermaphrodite; that this peculiar

form of Nature's freaks was by no means uncommon in
the country; and that all such people were obliged to dress
in female costume.[17]

The comments by Hallett and by Wood dispel any notion
that *kathoey* are a product of the tourist boom of the 1960s
and 1970s. They represent something much more deep rooted and mysterious than the 'ladyboy' entertainers. But what
are they? And what has been their traditional historical place
in the culture of Siam?

Dance

Today *kathoey* enjoy popularity as dancers, with the tourists,
with native Thai adults and notably in the smaller venues
with Thai children. Dance-theatre (the two are inseparable in
Thai performances) has played an important part in the cultural life of Siam for centuries, from the royal courts down to
the poorest, most rustic communities. It has various recognised forms. Could any of these be a precursor to the modern cabaret show? Is the modern cabaret something
completely new or are there whispers of older performance
traditions within it?

The three main forms of traditional dance-drama in
Thailand are *khon, lakhon nai* and *likay*. *Khon* and *lakhon
nai* each represent classical forms and originated exclusively
as court entertainments. Until the nineteenth century there
were no public theatres as such. Both are highly formal.
Khon is danced by masked performers and depicts scenes
from the *Ramakian* (the Thai version of India's *Ramayana*),
a moral tale about Prince Rama and a monkey army that is
set against the forces of evil. Performances are stylised, of
epic proportion and can go on for several days. They require
a huge cast with actors playing the roles of gods, giants, men,
monkeys, demons and beasts. The mask makers are considered artisans of the highest order. The less grandiose but
equally stylised *lakhon nai* was common amongst the lesser
courts. It is danced unmasked and may take its plot from a
number of legends. While the emphasis of *khon* is on

virtuosity, muscular power and sheer scale, that of *nakhon nai* is on beautiful costumes, grace and finely controlled movement, particularly of the hands and feet.

Lakhon nai was an important entertainment in the royal courts, the larger palaces often boasting a resident dance troupe. The nineteenth-century missionary, Herbert Warrington Smyth tells how the girl dancers in these troupes were expected to train from an early age 'especially in the practice of twisting their joints in a radical manner'. The best trained were to be found in the Bangkok palace where they 'spend all day exercising and practising picking up bits of straw with their eyelids . . . a highly structured "ballet" with sequences of hand movements and simultaneous agitation of many muscles of the body – like the flutter of leaves'.[18]

The academies of the formal *khon* dance were originally made up of men and those of the equally formal *lakhon nai* were made up of women although this is not necessarily the case in the performer of the present day. Descriptions of these different forms of dance by visitors to the royal courts make no mention of the presence of any performers of an ambiguous gender.

Likay, the third form of dance-theatre, was historically the property of the common people rather than that of royalty. It is a much more flexible entertainment that draws on various sources, including *lakhon nai*, but contains scope for improvisation, topical references and humour, often of a lewd and bawdy nature. Still popular at provincial temple festivals, at one time no country fair or celebration was considered complete without a *likay* show. With its emphasis on popular entertainment *likay* is obviously much more like the modern cabaret show than *khon* or *lakhon nai*. Could it perhaps be its ancestor?

Walter Irvine, a postgraduate student of London University's School of Oriental and African Studies, spent four years in rural villages in northern Thailand from 1977. He was interested in spirit worship, spirit possession and spirit media in these parts. His thesis[19] contains some fascinating photographs, one of which was taken in the town of Chiang Mai and is captioned, 'Members of a *likay* opera troupe sitting backstage before the figure of their teacher spirits'. It is clear that the individuals in the group are *kathoey* and also apparent that they are about to perform for a village audience and not in front of tourists. The attention they are paying to the image of 'teacher spirits' reflects their Animist legacy.

Much earlier, in 1900, Charles Buls,[20] a prominent Belgian mayor and travel writer of the day, also photographed the dancers in what he describes as a 'ballet', both on and off stage, see Plates 1 and 2 (between pages 86–87). Plate 1 shows the costumed performers on stage, and Plate 2 shows them enjoying a moment of relaxation off stage. Even off stage their appearance is that of ambiguous-gender people. These are the *kathoey* of the time. This fact is implicitly referred to in a later English translation of Buls' book where the photograph shown here as Plate 2 carries the caption, *'Actresses', as seen by Buls*. The parentheses are those of the translator. There is more than a passing resemblance of the costumed performers as they are pictured in Plate 1 to modern cabaret dancers (see Plate 4). Ensemble numbers such as 'Welcome to Thailand', which is part of the popular repertory of many modern venues, look very like the group in Plate 1. From his description, the performance Buls watched appears to have been a mixture of *lakhon nai* and *likay* forms.

Something else that took place during the performance that evening caught Buls' attention. He describes this as follows.

> During this performance I observed a remarkable scene in the neighbouring box. A lady of high rank called a Chinese usher from time to time who listened to her message on his knees and received a few pieces of money. A few minutes later the Chinese would reappear on the stage. He would crawl near one of the actors and give him the gift of our neighbour. The actor would first make a fuss but then interrupt his play, kneel and, with his hands joined above his head, abandon himself in prostration in honour of his generous admirer, without the public paying any attention to this *hors-d'oeuvre*.[21]

More or less exactly the same business of tipping a performer during the performance can be seen in the modern cabaret. It does not of course happen in the lavish hi-tech productions because any interruption to the tightly timed flow of effects would spoil the show. In these it is arranged that the tipping takes place after each performance. But in smaller-scale, more intimate venues, presenting a performer with a small note actually during the show is a regular practice. As in the performance that Buls watched, the recipient of a tip will respond with a prayer-like gesture of the hands and a small bow (*wai*). The episode usually gets a round of applause from the audience.

The first reference to *kathoey* performing in front of foreign visitors is in the cabaret bars that sprang up in Bangkok in the 1940s, during and after the Second World War. Demand for these was encouraged by a large occupying Japanese army who arrived in Thailand in 1941, and after they had gone when this war was won, an influx of allied troops, diplomats and officials. But the shows were equally popular among Siamese and Chinese. American official and journalist J. Orgibet[22] recalls that the shows typically involved dancers, orchestras, strippers and hostesses. And typically the 'show stopper' was a *kathoey*. These shows represent a half-way house between the often bawdy traditional folk entertainment designed for the ordinary folk of Siam and the modern cabaret and bar entertainment for the tourists.

The few images and accounts that exist enable the origins of the modern commercial 'ladyboy' cabaret to be pieced together and traced to the popular *likay* of the past. It is a similar style of theatre adapted to an evolving cosmopolitan audience. It is not a form of entertainment that has been suddenly thought up to supply a tourist market but one with a historical place and provenance in the culture of Siam. It is also evident that one of the traditional roles *kathoey* have held in the Siamese community is that of dancer and entertainer, not in the formal *khon* and *lakhon nai* dramas of the courts, but in the more burlesque style of performance and improvised entertainment that has been popular with the ordinary folk of the villages.

This notion of *kathoey* as entertainers of the common people is consistent with another role they enjoy within the
broader Thai community – that of participants in public
beauty competitions. Local festivals, or temple fairs, are held
annually in certain parts of central and northern Thailand
and often include a beauty contest in which the contestants
are all *kathoey*. Jeremy Marre's film *Ladyboys*, made for BBC
Channel 4 in 1992[23] includes coverage of one of these. There
is a first round involving several hundred contestants and a
second round in which the winners are picked from some fifty
finalists. These temple events are organised by committees of
monks not for tourists but for the local villages. They are
hugely popular and draw large numbers of high-spirited spectators who cheer, applaud and wolf-whistle the contestants as
they parade along a catwalk in their costumes.

Spirit Mediums and Healing

Anthropologists have sometimes remarked on an association
between shamanism, or spirit healing, and forms of transgender behaviour in countries as diverse as Siberia,
Indonesia, Philippines and parts of north and central
America.[24] Apart from their role in the community as public
entertainer, could there have been a tradition of *kathoey* as
village shaman?

In Animist communities, where spirits are held to be
responsible for rains, droughts, fertility and good and bad
fortunes of all kinds, it is not surprising to find spirits cited
as the agents responsible for the personal health or ill-health
of the individual. In the Animist tradition of Siam and its
neighbours, a person's health depends upon a balance
between the four elements: wind, fire, earth and water. In old
Siam, and still to this day in less developed parts of the country, there are four methods of diagnosing and treating an ill-
ess. Common ailments, like headache or cold, are treated in
 home with simple remedies such as diet, special herbs and
 sage. In more serious cases a doctor might be called in
 is a medically unqualified person but who is respected

as 'educated' by other members of the community. Historically, palm-leaf manuscripts have served as medical texts. The prescriptions of these men were of a similar kind to those dispensed by the doctors and quacks of medieval Europe; objects such as a piece of the jaw-bone of a wild hog, special roots gathered by moonlight, etc., and as with the European remedies, potency was related to the difficulty in procuring the ingredients that made up the cure.[25] These doctors were always men.

Should both these approaches fail, or if the person is the subject of an acute attack, the cause of the patient's illness is presumed to be possession by a spirit (*phii*), and a spirit doctor is sent for. There are many different types and categories of *phii* all credited with different origins and different degrees of potency and malignancy. The spirit doctor's task is to find out which spirit is responsible for the patient's sickness and the name of the person from whom the spirit was transferred. Lillian Curtis, an American missionary active in north Siam in the late nineteenth century, describes the proceedings thus:

> The doctor uses a light cane for flogging or a tiger's tooth for scratching the flesh while demanding the name of some person against whom there is a grudge or who is unpopular. The accused is sent for and the spirit transferred back to this witch whose property is destroyed and who is driven away from the village.[26]

These spirit doctors are also always men. Such a drastic procedure is clearly wide open to abuse. More commonly, and in cases where uncertainty exists as to what is wrong with the person a medium is called in. Curtis writes:

> These mediums are always women, as the spirit doctors are men . . . They sit in state upon a mat, and are given every attention by the waiting, expectant, family. If possible a native band of musicians is obtained who perform the whole time. Arrack (an alcoholic drink) is offered the medium and is partaken of freely. When it begins to

animate her she sways and chants improvised incantations, until she is seized by a spirit of inspiration and becomes frantic in her gestures and movements at which point the music swells to a tumult.

Questions are then asked about cause and cure in the medium's attempt to identify a spirit or spirits that may have been offended and how to propitiate them. Animist theories of spirits, spirit possession and the constant requirement to propitiate spirits are complex. The spirit medium does not herself wield power. She is a weak and passive vessel who enters a trance-like state during which her consciousness is obliterated and she is taken over by a spirit. The medium is *maa khii* – literally 'a horse to ride'. During this possession by her *chao*, or 'spirit mount' she is not held responsible for her actions. Everything she does and says is attributed to the spirit that possesses her. Consequently there is an implicit license to consume large amounts of alcohol and a temporary suspension of censorship of drunkenness, flirtation, lewd talk and any other form of behaviour that at other times would be regarded as socially unacceptable.

In Curtis's detailed account of these healing sessions in the north of the country during the late nineteenth century, the various categories of healer are clearly recorded as man or woman and there is no mention of any involvement of people of ambiguous gender.

Walter Irvine's[27] observations, however, give a rather different picture. His thesis contains several photographs of female and male mediums and also of male mediums dressed as women. These latter are wearing brightly coloured, even garish, skirts, blouses and head-dresses. Of the fifty-two mediums Irvine studied, thirty-four were females and of the remaining eighteen, thirteen are described by him as 'homosexual males'.

My own questioning of some of the older townsfolk of Chiang Mai yielded the unanimous response that mediumship has traditionally been the province of women and that the *kathoey* mediums are few and are relatively new to the scene.

Interestingly, Irvine observes that there had been a substantial increase in the number of people operating as spirit
mediums from the 1950s up until the time of his study in the
late 1970s. This is attributed to a certain dissatisfaction with
other forms of healing, coupled with an increase in the general wealth of the population at this time, on account of
money flowing to the north from the south as a result of the
tourist boom and in particular the sex trade. This increased
wealth may have attracted opportunist 'fake' practitioners;
'fake', that is, in the sense that their motives were driven
more by financial considerations than spiritual ones. Perhaps
the mediums described and photographed by Irvine wearing
woman's attire were newcomers to the scene who, like the
cabaret dancers whose numbers swelled during this time,
were *kathoey* seizing a commercial opportunity. The photographs show them as noticeably older and/or less attractive
than their performer counterparts. An uncharitable theory
might be that these are stateless individuals in search of a
niche, unemployed, unable to get jobs as performers and
rejected by communities of their own kind.

Indigenous transgender behaviour is most commonly
described by anthropologists in societies that remain domi-
nated by Animist beliefs. There is sufficient circumstantial
evidence to surmise that *kathoey* also have their origins in
Animism. Many *kathoey* appear to originate from the north
of the country where Animist traditions persist to a greater
degree than in the more developed regions of the south.
Among the *kathoey* in my sample, some form of belief in the
potency of spirits was universal. But what evidence there is
suggests that while a few *kathoey* may at the present time
perform as genuine spirit mediums this does not appear to
have been a core traditional role for them. The role of medium has been, and still is, predominantly the domain of
women. Unlike in some countries, for example the
Philippines, where transgendered people enjoy an identity as
mediums or spirit doctors, it would seem the historical identity of *kathoey* is to be found elsewhere; namely in the role
of public entertainer at festive and auspicious events.

Temporary Transformation

Sometimes in Animist spirit healing rituals a male medium may assume the guise of a woman purely for the duration of the trance session, reverting to their everyday male image afterwards.[28] A similar kind of short-term cross-dressing by males is a common feature of festivals in northern Thailand, especially the 'sky rocket' festivals (*bun bang fai*) that are held at the end of the hot season in May. The purpose of these events is to encourage the much needed rains and this is done by firing home-made rockets into the sky. Preparations take place within the normally peaceful setting of the temple, and teams compete with one another to see who can produce the biggest firework. On the day prior to the shooting of the rockets there is much dancing, singing and drunken revelry in the village. The rains are supposedly the result of a sexual union between the gods, and the dances and verses, performed mainly by men, are full of sexual innuendo. Travel writer William Klausner describes one such event,

> There is much gaiety in the village with song and dance, drinking and a great deal of sexual by-play with risqué songs, crude sexual pantomimes, boys dressed as girls and phallic symbols waved about. . . . It is a colourful spectacle with male costumes varying from the traditional tartan-like plaid sarong to a borrowed dress or skirt and a bandana tied around the head and grapefruit stuffed in the appropriate places. Men's faces are powdered and they emulate hand movements of *lakhon* with the copper finger-nails attached.[29]

Clearly there is a world of difference between a man who wants to have a bit of fun by dressing up as a women for a short while and the five-year-old boy who knows for certain that he wishes to spend his life as a girl, or at least as a *kathoey*. Nevertheless, the fact that cross-dressing is a regular feature of these occasions further highlights the association of gender plasticity, and the libertine absence of any machismo-like censorship of crossing male-female barriers, within Animist traditions.

Respect and Disdain

The odd mixture of respect and disdain that *kathoey* evoke in the general Thai public was very apparent during the time I spent with them. Not infrequently would a complete stranger comment quite spontaneously on a particular individual's beauty and then enter into a lengthy discussion of hair style or make up or even cosmetic surgery. It was noticeable that this was almost always a woman and always a person of lower or working-class status, a street vendor, waitress or housewife, to give a few examples. The disdainful looks seemed to come mainly from middle-class professionals.

American academic Eric Allyn thinks that, 'like the Filipino *bakla* and the *berdache* of certain North American tribes, the *kathoey* probably at one time had a special, honoured place in Thai society.[30] He supports this view by showing that many time-honoured and colloquial terms for *kathoey* reflect a degree of admiration in the general populus; *nang-fa jamlaeng* – a 'transformed angel', *norng-toey-nang-kor* – an affectionate term for a younger *kathoey* considered to be particularly attractive, *phuying praphet sorng* – a 'second kind of woman' and *sao dao-thiam* – 'satellite woman', a respectful term for a cabaret dancer.

In contrast to the traditionally positive attitude amongst ordinary Thai people which these colloquial terms would seem to reflect, recent years have seen *kathoey* come in for a certain amount of bad publicity accorded them by government propagandists as well as an increasing amount of harassment by the police. The growth of this new discrimination has proceeded hand in hand with the growth of the relative newcomer in Thai society – the middle-class professional. This change in tone can be put down to a keenness on the part of the authorities to promote their idealised vision of a more 'modern', Western style, sanitised Thailand; a Thailand with men and women and nothing in between – at the expense, it would seem, of a deep rooted cultural heritage. Here is a case of the authorities of a country turning against an ancient institution of its own for the sake of presenting what it naïvely supposes to be a more acceptable face to the outside world. The unfairness and hypocrisy of this recent policy is nicely highlighted in Jeremy Marre's film, *Ladyboys*, in which the ex-prime minister is seen enjoying the festivities in the exclusively Thai audience of an up-country *kathoey* beauty competition.[31]

Prostitution

Pre-marital sexual relations are disapproved of in Thai society but it is considered semi-legitimate (and is common practice) for a man to visit a prostitute. Peter Jackson has suggested a possible secular historical role for *kathoey* as providing a sexual outlet for young men before they marry,

> From the standpoint of traditional ritual sanctions, it would have been more acceptable for an unmarried youth to visit a *kathoey* than to have sex with an unmarried young woman, whose reputation would be sullied if she was discovered. Visiting a *kathoey* would also have been a safer sexual option for a village youth as he would not have to face the ire of a young woman's family if discovered ... Should this speculation on the historical role of the *kathoey* in rural Thai society be accurate, then the contemporary Thai stereotype of *kathoeys* as prostitutes may be based on more than misogynistic prejudice ... The common colloquial expression for *kathoeys*, 'a second type of woman' (*phu-ying praphet sorng*) appears to reflect this.[32]

Certainly of the forty-three *kathoey* I met and talked to in the course of my research, the majority could be described as sexual libertines and many had worked at some point in their lives as prostitutes, serving both Thai and *farang* customers. The image of the *kathoey* as prostitute, or at least as a person who is available for sex, is very much part of Thai folklore. Another obvious advantage in a Thai village youth visiting a *kathoey* rather than a girl lies in the fact that there is no chance of the encounter resulting in a pregnancy.

In their other traditional role as performers, more precisely as providers of dance and entertainment for festive occasions, they are not unlike the variety show girls of London and Paris in the nineteenth and early twentieth centuries. Both serve the purpose of bringing light escapist theatre to a people struggling under the burden of poverty or war. And in both cases the performers are notorious for their coquetry and general availability.

Love and a Broken Heart

It is very common to hear *kathoey* express romantic aspirations and bemoan the difficulty of finding the 'true love' (*kwam rak jing*) of a 'handsome' man. Failure to find love, happiness and stability in a long-term relationship is mythologised as the lot of a *kathoey*. As Jackson puts it,

> If the *kathoey's* historical role in Thailand has indeed been to provide men with a transitional sexual outlet until they marry, then the 'suffering' of living with a broken heart and the impossibility of finding lasting true love would appear to be the culturally ordained fate of *kathoeys* in traditional Thai society.[33]

This culturally ingrained representation finds expression in folk stories and dramas in which one or more of the characters is a *kathoey*. An example is the highly successful film *The Iron Ladies* (*Satree Lex*), which dramatises the true tale of the controversy that blew up when the Thailand National Volleyball champions in 1996 were a team made up entirely of *kathoey*. The film tracks the turbulent life of one of the members of the team, Pia, who is recruited from a career as a stage celebrity. She is shown in floods of tears as her Thai boyfriend deserts her for a girl – the classic 'broken heart' of the legend.[34]

There are many examples of the legend becoming reality. Suicides, suicide attempts and hysterical reactions are considerably more common among *kathoey* than in the wider population. The wrist scars and other self-inflicted wounds among them bear witness to this as do the not infrequent newspaper reports of successful suicide attempts. In the Buddhist tradition the life of a *kathoey* is a life of punishment, a prison sentence from which there can be no remission in this life. The only glimmer of light is the hope of redemption in the next. There is even an unspoken tradition amongst those who see themselves as condemned concerned with the method of suicide; the two preferred procedures are stabbing oneself and/or jumping from a tall building.

For the unfortunate *kathoey* life is cheap and emotions often run high. Explosions of temper are said to be the result of two people ill at ease with each other within the one body. Too much to drink reputedly results either in this reaction or in one of hysterical weeping.

Conclusion

There are clear indications that *kathoey* have for a long time been an indigenous part of the culture of Thailand and old Siam. Northern Thai origin legends suggest that the pre-modern Thai sex/gender system was based on a model of the three genders: male, female and *kathoey*. They did not start life as the 'ladyboys' of the late twentieth-century cabaret shows. They appear to have enjoyed a historical role in old Siam as popular entertainers. It does not stretch credulity to see the modern cabaret show as an adaptation of these older forms of dance and performance to a modern cosmopolitan audience.

Neither, it appears, are *kathoey* primarily a product of Hindu or Buddhist religions. They, along with indigenous transgendered minorities in many other cultures that we might call 'primitive', most likely have their origins in archaic communities in which Animism and the worship of spirits lay at the core of everyday beliefs and rituals. Such communities pre-date the arrival on the cultural scene of a more formal, doctrinaire religion. In Thailand this was to be Buddhism which, far from criticising and rejecting the old Animist beliefs, amalgamated with them to create the new religious order. As Buddhism embraced and to some extent incorporated many Animist traditions, the scriptural texts show that it also embraced and incorporated the Animist legacy of *kathoey*, or *phet thi-sam* – a 'third sex'.

Chapter 7
Lek's Story

It is common practice for declared *kathoey* to begin taking oestrogen-based hormones around the age of puberty in order to enhance the femininity of their features and to encourage the development of breasts. Lek, along with her friends, started this at the age of fourteen.

Unlike some fourteen-year-old boys who announce their intention of becoming girls, or *kathoey*, Lek had had no major problem with her family accepting her new identity. Her father had disappeared when she was four and she had no memory of him. She lived with her mother, an aunt, her grandmother and her younger sister. She had never made any special effort to conceal an interest in make-up and girls' clothes which had made itself apparent at an early age. Her mother was by no means stupid and had picked up on these signs when Lek was at primary school.

She had kept her old name just as she had told Saowanee she would that day of their first meeting at Saowanee's apartment. 'Lek' in Thai means small and can be the name of a boy or a girl. Unlike the others she had not grown her hair long immediately after her initiation as a *kathoey*. She kept it short in the cause of playing volleyball. However, by the time she captained the school team in her final year, it was shoulder-length and she would play the game wearing a head-band.

Of the three school friends Lek came from the poorest family, whose meagre income was provided by her mother and her aunt working the rice fields, while Grandmother tended to the home and its smallholding. Rice, coconuts, wild fruit and eggs from their four hens plus the occasional purchase of poor meat from a villager who worked at the Chiang Mai slaughterhouse were the main ingredients of their monotonous diet. The family could not afford to pay for Lek to go to university, although this is what she would have liked. She wanted to study electronic engineering and afterwards get a decent job in this marketable field so as to be able to fulfil the traditional duty of a daughter by supporting her family.

After leaving school, at seventeen, she combed the city looking for any kind of work and for two and a half years had temporary jobs as cleaner at a large hotel, kitchen assistant at another, helper at a hairdressing salon and receptionist/secretary at a photographic studio in the multi-storey Central Store next to the Chiang Mai Orchid Hotel. The hotel jobs involved long hours and pitiful pay. The hairdresser and the photographer paid little better but she enjoyed the work because the staff were fun and there were often other *kathoey* around. In between these various jobs she helped her mother and her aunt on the farm. Their mentor and 'sister' Saowanee had warned the friends that getting a job was not easy for a *kathoey*, but Lek had not believed her. Lek was bright and carried with her a good report from the school. But she was to discover that many of the big employers such as the hotels, banks and offices would not even consider her and the ones that would offered work that was poorly paid and hidden away from the public.

In Thailand, as in most other countries in the world, there are many practices that are carried on quite openly but that are technically illegal. Gambling and bribery are two examples. Although such practices are commonplace, officially they do not exist. The same duality exists in respect of attitudes to the *kathoey* population. It is not illegal to be a *kathoey* and this category of person is universally (if tacitly) acknowledged as integral to the culture and as part of the cultural heritage. But a similar coyness exists amongst those professional classes that must present a formal, or official, front to the public about openly acknowledging that they are present as part of normal, everyday life. Many of these people are reluctant to speak about *kathoey* and seem almost to treat it as a taboo subject. This is especially so among those elements of Thai society who regard themselves as on the cutting edge of economic and cultural advancement through 'modernisation', Western style. And these, for the main part, are the people in control of recruitment for the new generation of jobs that are far more lucrative than working in the fields. In rural villages, insulated from the economic pressures of industrialisation, where the community remains tight-knit and low profile, it is natural and unproblematical for them to be openly accepted as members of that community. But in the developing parts of the country where a demand for commercial expertise, professional services and a cosmopolitan image dictates the cultural scene, they seem to have become something of an embarrassment. While their ubiquitous presence cannot be kept a secret, there is a certain will amongst those Thais who consider themselves to be international in their outlook to deny them a role in the general community of modern Thailand and (nominally at least) consign them to the domains of cabaret and entertainment, as if these are and always have been their only legitimate places of employment.

The two jobs Lek was offered that did involve contact with the public, and the only two that didn't feel like slavery – in the hairdressing salon and the photographic studio – were both acquired with the help of friends and contacts. Entering good and secure employment is difficult enough for an ordinary girl leaving a Chiang Mai secondary school and it could be argued that the prejudice Lek ran up against was to some extent balanced by the contacts she was able to activate through the sorority of *kathoey* and its networks. Of Lek's contemporaries at school only the very bright ones achieved funding for further education or were able to enter at the bottom of a career ladder on their own merit and without the help of a friend of the family in a position of influence. But the difficulty in breaking out of the poverty trap is compounded for *kathoey* owing to the prejudice against them of many employers and the restricted areas of employment for which they are generally considered eligible.

Lek's enthusiasm for sport, especially volleyball, remained undiminished and to some extent kept her sane through these difficult years of grubbing around for whatever work she could get. She formed her own team of six friends and they would play other teams from the local villages as often as it was possible to get together.

By 1995 Lek was nineteen. In this year a story was brewing in the national press which made her and many others throughout the country sit up. This was the reporting of a volleyball team in the town of Lamphang – some 100 kilometres south-east of Chiang Mai – that was gaining a reputation for winning all its fixtures and was rumoured to be invincible. Nothing startlingly newsworthy about this fact on its own. But this team was unique in that five out of its six players were *kathoey*. The team who called themselves *Satree Lex*, or 'The Iron Ladies', had had a turbulent recent history. It started with Mon, a highly rated sports person, being refused admission to the team not on account of ability but purely because he/she was a *kathoey*. Later on a new coach was appointed by the local governor who was more open minded so Mon, together with her friend Jun, were not discouraged to reapply for trials for the team and were selected in the final list of players. This caused an uproar among the male members of the team all of whom, except the vice-captain, Chai, walked out. But Mon and Jun quickly gained control and selected three of their friends, all excellent players and all *kathoey*, to make up the rest of the team.

This was a bold move on the part of the minority group. It was to pay off. They had struck out against and successfully overturned a decision based on prejudice. But perhaps even more important, they had attracted considerable national publicity. Here was a flood of news stories that openly acknowledged not only the existence of *kathoey* in the community at large but also portrayed this particular group as a talented and courageous bunch of individuals. Naturally this caused a certain embarrassment among the more conservative officials who sat on the committees that organised matches and competitions. These people found themselves in an awkward position. The team from Lamphang was now officially constituted, apparently very successful and attracting a great deal of publicity. It was too late to attempt any form of veto or censorship. The players

1. *Kathoey* dancers in late 19th century Siars.

2. 'Actresses' relaxing off-stage, as seen by Buls.

3. Siamese woman in the 1890s.
Note the similarity in appearance to the *Kathoey* actresses.

4. A modern 'ladyboy' caberet performer.

5. A modern 'ladyboy' poses for a press slot. (The string around her left wrist is a Buddhist Blessing).

6. 'Rosepaper' warming up for a show.

already had a growing popular following. The climax to the story came the following year, 1996, when a last-ditch attempt to discredit the team was made by allowing them to participate in the Thailand National Male Volleyball Competition, but giving them three straight games to play on the first day of the National League. Their detractors hoped that they would be eradicated and thereafter fade into obscurity. Instead the team confounded the bureaucrats by winning all three games. This of course made them more popular than ever.

This story was causing something of a national sensation not so much on account of the sporting prowess of the team but because here was a national news-piece about *kathoey* right in people's faces which not only brazenly flouted the unspoken taboos about the public acknowledgement of such people but presented them in an up-beat manner as celebrities!

Four years later these events were to be followed by a final act of daring when Thai film director Yongyoot Thongkongthun made a feature film that told the story of the volleyball team and its struggles against the odds to gain recognition. The film was called *Satree Lex* after the team.[1] Days before the release of the film in the year 2000 producers at Tai Entertainment warned the young director that audiences might give the film a bad reception. Never in the history of Thai cinema had a film been released in which *kathoey* were portrayed as real people with hearts and minds and a significant presence in the wider community. The conspiratorial cover was at last blown. Said thirty-three-year-old Yongyoot, 'I broke all the taboos in the business'.

To the surprise and delight of the producers the film – essentially a comedy with a sympathetic personal angle – it turned out to be a major box-office success with something of a cult following. People were flocking to the cinemas and many were returning to see the film more than once. Within ten days it had pulled in 60 million Baht (about £1m), considerably more than it had cost to make, and was on the way to being the second biggest ever box-office hit in the history of Thai film-making.

Immediately she learned about the team Lek dreamed of being a part of it, maybe as a reserve player. Coming up was a home match between the *Satree Lex* team and a visiting team from the south. Lek set about saving up enough money for the coach fare and a ticket for the match and made the journey to Lamphang to be a spectator. After the match she planned to approach the coach to see if there was any possibility of a trial with the team as a reserve. She watched the game with a mix of excitement and sadness. The stadium was packed with noisy and enthusiastic spectators and it was impossible not to pick up on the buzz that gripped the crowd. Both teams were made up of top players and it very soon became uncomfortably clear to Lek that she was not in the same league. She was a good local player, but she had neither the height nor the dexterity of these amazing professionals and seeing them realised it would be pointless to approach the team for a trial. That night she travelled back home dejected but nevertheless determined to change direction in some way. She could not carry on the way she was in Chiang Mai, moving from one uncertain and poorly paid job to the next. She would go south to Bangkok and find work there. Several of her friends had done this and were now sending regular instalments of money back to their families in their home villages of the north. Som, who had been her 'sister' at the school in Chiang Mai, together with Saowanee, was one of them so she would visit Som and ask her advice. The excitement of the *Satree Lex* episode, despite her dashed ambition to be part of the team, had sparked in her a determination for change.

The decision taken, Lek wasted no time in handing in her notice to the photographic studio where she was working and telling her mother. Her mother and all the other mothers in the villages of the north knew only too well what happened to undeducated girls coerced to migrate to the south. But Lek was not uneducated and was not acting under coercion. Her friend Som had found reasonably paid (by Chiang Mai standards anyway) work as a waitress/cook in a smart area of the city and Lek assured her mother that she would land something similar which would enable her to send money home on a regular basis.

Bangkok

When I started learning Thai I was surprised to find the Thai
term *rot tit*, meaning traffic jam, so frequently used in
examples of everyday talk. First time in Bangkok and I soon
understood why. At certain times of the day the city gets so
strangled with traffic that taxi drivers may refuse to accept
fares from some districts to others. Lek had been warned
about the traffic but nothing had quite prepared her for the
monstrous walls of cars and motorcycles that ground their
way through the city. She spent twenty minutes wondering
how to cross the sixteen-lane Thanon Ratchadamnoen where
the vehicles crawled on without stopping and there were no
subways. She soon learned the technique by studying other
Thais of walking *into* the oncoming traffic and kind of weav-
ing a path between the vehicles which would respond by
minutely slowing down giving you just enough time to dodge
through to the next one. This trick she would in due course
pass on to me.

Alas the traffic was not the only shock the city would provide. It was far from the land of plenty that she had expected. Lek first of all went to see her friend Som who, sure
enough, through a web of contacts, had got herself a good
job in the kitchen of an upmarket restaurant on the
Sukhumvit Road. The hours were long and the work tiring.
But she earned enough to be able to pay for a small room
which she shared with a friend and to send a little money
back to her family in the north. Som told Lek that she could
stay with herself and her room mate until she found work,
but this must be on a short-term basis only as the room was
too small for the three of them.

There were no vacancies in the restaurant where Som
worked but Som had heard that the bars and restaurants in
the Khao San Road, Banglamphoo – the traveller's Mecca –
were a fruitful hunting ground and she took time off work to
take Lek to this throbbing tourist's terminus and introduce
her to some of the managers of these busy establishments.
Sure enough there was work here and, although it paid less
than half of what Som earned, Lek took it and spent the next
months as a waitress in a cybercafé that closed at 3.30 in the

morning and was a popular watering-hole for a constant stream of sweaty backpackers.

Such was Lek's introduction to the big city. She made new friends, in particular Pai who worked at the same café, and after a few weeks she moved out of Som's room at the other end of town into an even smaller room that she and Pai had agreed to share and that room was just three minutes' walk from the cybercafé.

Lek's lot was no more or less fortunate than that of other girls from the north who had completed a secondary education and then come to Bangkok to find work. She was not cut out for office work. She liked the banter with the backpackers and she grew to like Bangkok in spite of the traffic. The German manager of the cybercafé was fair in respect of the hours she was expected to work although the pay was low. Compared with younger less educated girls who were trafficked from their villages and bonded into what virtually amounted to slave labour at one of the textile factories or in one of the many closed brothels serving Thai and Chinese customers, she had it fairly good. She was even learning to speak some English.

After eighteen months working in the Khao San Road she made the journey north to visit her family and friends. She had not been unhappy working at the café but the money she was paid did not leave anything over for her to send back home. After Bangkok, village life seemed incredibly quaint and slow moving. Her mother, grandmother and sister were all well but she was disturbed to see how much her aunt had aged during this short time. Now she was able to tackle only light work on the farm and Lek could see that her mother was struggling. Although her mother did not refer to it directly, Lek could tell she was disappointed at not receiving money because of the veiled references to 'other girls' from the village who were working in the south and sending regular payments to their families. It is a Thai tradition, indeed a duty, for daughters to support their families if they can. They are expected to pay back the 'breast milk' given to them as babies.

She returned to Bangkok feeling guilty and knowing that

she would have to try to find better paid work. Pai, her room-mate had often talked of the *farang* bars in the Patpong area of the city and the sizeable sums of money some of the girls who worked there apparently received. Patpong is notorious as a pick-up place for sex tourists, but Pai told Lek that by no means all of the bar girls worked as prostitutes – some merely talked to the customers so as to make them feel welcome and made sure they never had an empty glass. If a customer offered to buy you a drink you would charge them seventy or eighty baht and some of this money you got to keep. So Lek and Pai decided they would investigate the scene at Patpong.

Four parallel streets make up the four acres of Patpong. Formerly a banana plantation owned by the Bank of Indochina the land was sold to the Hainanese-Thai family, Patpongphanit, in the late 1930s. Its bars started to appear in the 1940s as places of entertainment for airline staff from some fifteen offices that were established after the war. But it was not until the 1960s, when it became a favourite place of recreation for American GIs that it really began to grow and transform into the heaving tourist attraction it is today. The streets start to come alive about 8 p.m. when the scaffold stalls of the night market are being noisily set up. Numerous go-go, or floor-show bars speckle the district and these start getting into gear around 10 p.m., by which time the place is teeming with shoppers, drinkers, eaters (this is hardly the place for diners), voyeurs, punters and touts of all descriptions. The screeching calls of the bar girls is always the same – 'Hello, welcome. Where you from?, What your name? Where you go? Sit here please . . .'

Lek and Pai familiarised themselves with the area and spent time talking to the managers and the girls that worked at the bars. The go-go bars were pick-up joints where semi-naked girls paraded on a walkway with numbers pinned to their hips while tourists, men and women of all nationalities, sat around tables or right up at the walkway itself and inspected the merchandise. Many just came just to stare at the girls but some men would select a particular girl either for 'short time' in one of the rooms hidden away at the back of the building or 'long time' which meant overnight in the customer's hotel room. It was clear that some of the girls in these places, especially the younger ones, were less than enthusiastic about their work. Lek wondered about the circumstances and conditions under which they were employed. One place, King's Castle 3, was staffed exclusively with *kathoey* and the atmosphere was lively. The people who worked here seemed to be having a lot more fun than the girls in some of the other bars. But it was not Lek's scene.

Then there were the more ordinary bars, most of them run by Europeans or Americans, that did not offer any kind of floor show. These were semi open-air watering holes for the wandering foreigners. The Swedish owner and manager of one of these, the Green Papaya, was very interested to talk to Lek and Pai because they were attractive people with vivacious personalities and they spoke some English. These are qualities that can tempt a thirsty punter into one bar rather than another. He said he could offer them both work. He said that this need involve nothing more than just chatting to customers, serving them drinks and sitting on one of the stools close to the main tourist thoroughfare. There were loads of girls doing this, smiling at the passers by, trying to get their business. They were the advertisements for their particular establishment and, as any experienced bar owner knows, some are more effective advertisements than others.

As the girls work semi-freelance their earnings are to some extent up to them. They would be offered a low fixed monthly fee as a retainer for their loyalty to the Green Papaya, and they would receive a share of the profits from the drinks that customers bought for them. If a customer wanted to take them out, or 'off them', as this was known, that was up to the them, but he must pay a 'bar fine' to the management for the privilege. The amount of this fine varied from place to place. In the Papaya it was 450 baht (about £7). However, the manager, who had a Thai wife, insisted that his establishment was not primarily a venue for selling sex. Tourists came here for a drink and most of them enjoyed just chatting with an attractive Thai girl whose job it was to keep them happy and keep the drinks flowing so they did not feel inclined to move on to a different bar. The art was to turn what might have been a quick beer into five or six rounds, and this is what kept these businesses going. The manager of Papaya imposed a strict rule that only soft drinks could be bought for the girls. He said that often customers invite the girls out for a meal, a show or a disco as companions for the evening and no more than this. And yes, he admitted, sometimes they wanted more. It was up to the individual girl to assess a customer's intentions but very rarely did he have any problems. It was also up to the individual girl to fix a price for her services whatever these might be. This money she could keep. If a girl goes with a customer for whatever reason the customer must of course pay the bar fine as he is effectively hiring a girl and removing her temporarily from her place of work. The bar management and staff would, so far as they could, look after its girls by helping them find accommodation (Patpong is a long way from the Khao San Road), dealing with any troublesome or drunken customers and giving whatever other help and advice they were able. Good-looking young *kathoey* were considered an asset to these bars. Experience had shown that they attracted trade.

Lek and Pai checked with the girls who worked at Papaya that the facts the manager had given them were *bona fide*, as indeed they were. The European and American owners of this style of bar were generally respected by the girls who worked for them and Swedish Lars was reckoned to be one of the most honest and easy going. They looked at the fashionable clothes and jewellery the girls were wearing and they were decided. Both gave notice the following day at the cybercafé. They lost no time in moving from their place near the cybercafé on the Khao San Road to a room in a fairly quiet back street with a small balcony where clothes could be hung up to dry. There was no separate bathroom. A tiny toilet and shower had been improvised in one corner of the room by means of a wooden partition which stopped a foot short of the ceiling. In just two weeks they had become Patpong girls.

The Slope

Slippery or not, it is a common enough tale. A girl takes a job in a bar such as Papaya, fully intending not to sell sex at any cost. But prostitution is *de rigueur* in Patpong and considered a normal, everyday practice in the community of those who work there. Once living and working in this environment, over time a person becomes immured to the stigma that attaches to selling your body in the respectable world outside.

After only six weeks Lek accepted an invitation to go 'long time' – that is overnight – with a Frenchman she had met three days ago. No coercion whatsoever exists, at least at Papaya, for a girl to sell sex, but the forces are there, in place, waiting to tempt, and extremely hard to resist, especially when there is pressure to send money home to help your family, and especially if your family is in dire straits, as was Lek's when her aunt's health deteriorated yet further, so that she was unable to undertake any kind of work on the farm. It's all very well getting a share of the drinks that customers buy you, and the small regular monthly payments help, but the serious money is earned from entertaining a customer. For over a month Lek had been watching her well-dressed companions return from their assignations with money in their wallets and sometimes a gift of clothing chosen from one of the Western-style fashion shops. They seemed none the worse off. Lek didn't even own a wallet. Pai had lasted only ten days and Lek looked like a poor relation in the company of her friend.

Emile was on holiday from France for three weeks and had taken Lek to dinner at a fine fish restaurant on Sukhumvit Road. Lek had to borrow an evening dress from one of the others. After dinner Emile had returned alone to his hotel without propositioning Lek. Initially he did not know that Lek was a *kathoey*. Lek liked him and over dinner she had told him the truth. The flustered Emile only partially succeeded in hiding his dismay, but this was a land full of surprises and he refused to allow the strange news to spoil the evening. They enjoyed a great meal of fish chosen fresh from tanks and white wine, two glasses of which nearly made Lek pass out. She had mixed feelings about not being invited to the hotel that night. In one sense she was relieved – her principles still intact – and in another she was disappointed. Was it because she was a *kathoey*? Two days later, another dinner with wine, this time followed by a night in the posh Landmark Hotel, 2,000 baht in her pocket, a new pair of shoes, her principles out of the window and she felt great!

Such is the fate of many a well-intentioned country girl from the impoverished north and north-east of Thailand. Lek's aunt was now very ill and, needless to say, Lek's mother was more than pleased to start receiving regular lumps of cash and, as is the norm in poor families, she did not ask too many questions about where the money came from.

Three Years On

Three years was the longest period of time Lek had ever worked at a job. During this time she had seen many girls at the Green Papaya come and go, including her friend Pai who had married a Japanese man she met at the bar. Pai and her husband were now living in Tokyo. Lek still lived in the same rented room with the toilet in the corner that she had moved into with Pai, but she now shared it with her sister, who had moved to Bangkok from the north and worked as a packer on one of the huge prawn farms to the south of the city. By now Lek considered herself an old hand. Seventeen girls worked at the bar of whom two, Lek and one other were *kathoey*.

I am sitting with Lek on a bench in a park in a suburb of Bangkok that includes Dusit zoo. She likes to come here to be quiet for a few hours and to get away from the noise and smell of the Bangkok traffic. I have known Lek now for nearly a month. She knows I am writing a book and I have her confidence. The preceding account, and the following one, is Lek's story as it has unfolded in our many conversations (I won't say 'interviews'). Unprompted, she now tells me the tale of Big Mitch. She speaks of their encounter in some detail and knowing her as I do I find myself mentally filling in the gaps.

Big Mitch

As soon as Big Mitch walked into the Green Papaya and saw
Lek's curious round face, black eyes and tossing hair he was
taken. It took Lek less than a second to know this. When you
have worked in a bar like this for three years you cultivate
the skills of a cat, constantly scanning, knowing exactly your
field, all the time appearing preoccupied and disengaged.

She listened as he ordered a drink. American – a good
start. Fat, balding and past middle age – not so good but
common enough. Never mind, maybe he has *chai dii* – a
'good heart', that's what really counts. And money, of course.
She waited for him to settle, take stock of his surroundings,
light up a cigarette and take the first sip of his whiskey and
water. The situation is difficult if the stools either side of the
target are occupied. Not so in this case. On his right sat a
French couple and the stool to his left was free. Without hes-
itation she slipped on to the empty stool, faced him and
smiled. That was the beginning.

For the next eleven months he would see her as often as his
commitments back home in Chicago would allow. He made
three return visits to Thailand during this time, the first two
times staying with Lek for one month and the third time staying for three. He had no idea at first that Lek was a *kathoey*
– her camouflage was complete in that all the other bar girls
working on that particular night were girls. In due course he
would discover her secret but, after the initial shock, he was
surprised to find that it didn't matter. He had fallen for her
and respected her identification as a woman and proceeded
to continue to treat her as such.

Kathoey prostitutes who have not undergone full sex-
change surgery will use a variety of tricks in an attempt to
conceal their ambiguity from 'short time' customers. When
they are with someone on a longer-term basis they have to
expect mixed reactions from men who are initially naïve
about their sexual identity. There are ways of gauging a person's reaction. Lek had learned from her own experience
that, in most cases, even when it provoked an initial reaction
of alarm and reappraisal, her declared identity as a *kathoey*
did not stop a liaison from going ahead. There are many

examples of *farang* with a history of heterosexual tastes finding themselves in this situation, accepting it and going on to have long-term relationships with a *kathoey*, although some insist on paying for full sex-change or sex, reassignment surgery (SRS).[2]

Big Mitch was a consultant engineer for a construction conglomerate based in Chicago and it was his work that had brought him to Thailand. At sixty-two he was semi-retired and he had a wife and three grown-up sons back home all with families of their own. He was a generous man and throughout his liaison with Lek he made her a standing order of $US2,000 every month whether or not he was actually with her in Thailand. For a bar worker this was like striking gold. The Swedish owner of the Green Papaya paid the girls who worked there 2,400 baht (£40) a month and this was considered generous. The earnings they received from private arrangements with customers was variable, unpredictable and seasonal. Lek now had access to more money than she had ever dreamed of. She sent a third of this to her mother in the north, gave a third to her sister with whom she now shared a room in a suburb of Bangkok, bought herself a mobile phone and a camera and bought presents for her friends. The giving of gifts is a time-honoured practice in Thailand. Of significance is not so much the material value of the gift itself, nor even the thought behind it, but specifically the *act* of giving and the respect it commands and kammic credit that it accrues for the giver.

Lek would have liked to have continued her education after school. Her two school friends, Akorn and Manat, had both gone to universities. Their families or friends were able to support them over this time but Lek's was not. She had wanted to train as an electronic engineer and still harboured remnants of this ambition. Perhaps she would ask Mitch, but not just yet. There was something else she wanted, now with increasing urgency, and this was breast implants. She had been taking oral hormones now for nearly ten years and this had furnished her with distinct but small breasts. Her doctor had told her that ten to fourteen years was long enough. She had no desire to undergo total SRS but she felt the need for the more feminine shape that larger breasts would give her. If it came to a choice between further education and new breasts she would take the breasts.

Big Mitch turned out to have *chai dii*, sure enough. He was a good-hearted construction man with a fat belly and a fat wallet. They ate at the best restaurants in Bangkok. They went to the islands Ko Samui and Ko Phi Phi together. And they went to Chiang Mai, Lek's home town, though they did not visit Lek's family. Lek was disappointed that during their time together Mitch made no attempt at all to speak Thai. And at times she prayed for a spell that would make him less obese. But she was a dutiful companion to him and played her part honourably and with considerable grace and some moments of pleasure.

In the evenings Mitch liked to have a beer and a cigarette before dinner. He was to discover that, like most *kathoey*, Lek was extremely vain and needed more than an hour to make up and dress. So, whatever hotel they were in that evening, he would leave her to it and go down to the bar and wait for her to join him. This arrangement, under which each person had some time to themselves, suited them both well. It became a daily routine. Lek could telephone her family or friends if she so wished and Mitch would drink and maybe chat with other *farangs*, if there were any, at the bar, whilst waiting for Lek. After an excessive attention to detail in the bedroom mirror Lek would come down and sweep into the bar knowing that every pair of eyes in the place would be turned on her, some female ones less than charitably. Then, invariably, she would stroll over with exaggerated femininity to Mitch and greet him with the words, 'Beautiful darling, or not?' He got a thrill out of this quirky little ritual and grew to anticipate her entrance with relish.

Such was the pattern of their life together for the eleven months, on and off, which was to be the duration of their relationship.

But one day Mitch sat at the bar waiting for Lek as usual and she did not make her customary entrance. It was his third trip to Thailand to visit Lek and they had gone together to the lovely island, Ko Samui. The 'hotel' consisted of a collection of well-equipped individual bungalows up from a quiet beach, each with its own wooden veranda and its own spectacular view through coconut trees and other palms out over the ocean.

Big Mitch, sitting in the open-air bar that was a small distance up the hill from the bungalow where they were both staying, finished his fourth beer and looked anxiously down. Still there was no sign of Lek. He walked down the steep wooden steps that led there from the bar.

A knock on the door gave no answer. He tried the handle. The door was not locked and it swung open. There was no sign of Lek. He strode inside, concerned now. The place consisted of two air-conditioned rooms – a large bedroom and a bathroom – but Lek was not to be found in either. He wondered whether by some variant of sod's law she had walked a different route to the bar and their paths had crossed blindly. He sat on the bed and thought.

Then he saw her through the window, sitting on the veranda, upright and still. He stood up, walked to the door giving on to the veranda and opened it. There were two chairs and a table. They looked down on a cluster of decorative palm trees and through them the night sea. He sat down on the empty chair.

'What's up, babe?' he asked her.

'Tomorrow we go back Bangkok,' The great American jaw dropped.

'Trees say, darling.'

'WHAT!'

Lek made no reply. Mitch tried the trees for some sort of a clue and although he didn't understand and never would, he had a faint inkling of what she meant. The gigantic leaves danced, bowed, waved, shook hands in the breeze. Did they mock him? He thought of Chicago. Never had he felt so far from the back-slapping camaraderie of his friends back home. What the hell was he doing sitting in this place listening to a girl who was not a girl interpret the movements of the trees?

For Lek it was straightforward. The small jungle was the work of old Animist hands.[3] Its symmetry was potent and the spirits of the trees had spoken. They spoke of her sister and the little room in which they both lived with its small balcony and tiny toilet in the corner whose flimsy walls stopped short of the ceiling. They spoke of the emptiness of these hotels, of big money, and they were sending her home, back to her friends, Patpong and the Papaya Bar.

'Sorry, I gi' back money . . .'

She could see the words stung the American. Was it over? Would they travel to Bangkok the next day? Would he take the next available plane home and would they not see each other again?

'No, no, that's out of the question. Keep the money. I don't need it. Listen, it's OK. I understand. We both go home, and maybe I see you another . . .' This was no good and he knew it.

'I really would like to give you some more money for all the good times we've had. There have been good times, yes?'

'Good time, yes. No more money.'

'At least let me buy you something tomorrow. Some jewellery maybe.'

'Thank you. No jewellery. No more presents.'

There was nothing left for either of them to say and they sat in silence for a long time while the trees continued to perform their complex dances. Mitch thought of the last year and wondered what their times together had meant and whether they had any value. Did this all boil down to merely paying a prostitute for her services? It didn't feel like it. How can a Westerner ever get into the minds of these people? How impossibly different from his own culture and background. Out of the corner of his eye he saw Lek shed a silent tear. His reaction was one of relief – it could not have meant nothing to her after all. Could it?

Eventually Lek turned her round unmade-up face towards him, contorted with enquiry.

'Beautiful, darling, or not?'

This is the scene that flashed itself in front of me sitting on the park bench in Dusit listening to Lek's detailed account of her liaison with Mitch. She spoke in a serious tone both in

English and in Thai. I noticed that she spoke about him not without a degree of affection – he had *chai dii*: a good heart. It was also plain that it was she who had ended their relationship even though this meant the cessation of what must have been an incredible income for the time it lasted. Altogether she received eleven instalments of $2,000, i.e. $22,000. She told me there was nothing at all left of this money and I believed her. It was not that she was extravagant. Almost all of it had gone in gifts. I speculated, perhaps a little cynically, that she must have notched up considerable kammic credit over this period.

Lek told me that Mitch went back to the USA but he did not let go He kept the payments coming for another two months, sending flattering and imploring e-mails and making frequent attempts to contact her on her mobile. For Lek the thing was categorically over and she changed her telephone number when the calls kept on coming. Still he did not give up and when she received an e-mail some months later announcing his intention to return to Thailand she became sufficiently worried that she moved with her sister from the room with the toilet in the corner whose walls stopped short of the ceiling into a room in another part of the town. If he tried to find her at the bar they would cover for her and tell him she had left Bangkok.

It was starting to get dark and there were mosquitoes to which I knew Lek had a particular aversion. I thanked her for telling me the story of Mitch and suggested we go for a meal, but not at the expensive fish restaurant on the Sukhumvit Road. There was enough time before she returned to her shift later that night at the Green Papaya bar.

Chapter 8
The Sex Industry in Thailand

Tourist guides to the country will tell you that Thailand's is an export-led economy and that about 60 per cent of its exports are agricultural, with rice at the top of the list, followed by tapioca, coconut, rubber, tinned pineapple and products of the vast prawn fields south of Bangkok. Manufactured goods are increasingly important – in particular, textiles, cement and electronic products. From the 1980s through to 1997 Thailand had one of the fastest growing economies in the Pacific Rim. But in 1997 the boom turned to bust throughout south-east Asia, with Thailand, Indonesia, Malaysia, Philippines and South Korea the worst affected.

Notwithstanding the crash of 1997, for thirty years *per capita* income had seen a steady rise, especially in the towns, and extreme poverty was virtually eliminated. But by Western standards wages at the bottom of the scale are still low. The big money lies in land and property and this is in the hands of a comparatively small number of Thais and Chinese.

Whatever the tourist guides would have us believe, no one, not even the authorities, would privately deny that prostitution is a flourishing industry in Thailand and is probably more significant, in economic terms, than anything else. Estimates of the percentage of the gross national product from sex workers range from 2 per cent to a staggering 14 per cent. These estimates vary widely because no account is kept of how much cash actually changes hands. But few would dispute that money from the sex industry has contributed more to the development of towns in rural areas than all government programmes combined. The transformation of Chiang Mai from a small trading town in the north, with its temples as its focal points, to a city of frenetic markets and high-rise concrete buildings is primarily the result of a steady inflow of money from the south that was the proceeds of prostitution.

The Roots of Sex Tourism

Polygamy has been part of everyday life in Siam from the earliest days. The royal courts traditionally maintained harems of many concubines. Lesser citizens, if they could afford it, maintained 'second' and 'third' wives. Indeed, so commonplace was this practice that there was no word in the Siamese language that could translate the term 'polygamy'. In 1934 King Rama VII issued a law forbidding it. From the early 1900s It had become fashionable for the kings of Siam to seek an education in the West, and so it was finally conceded that the country's image needed modernising and bringing in line with what was seen as the cutting edge of the civilised world. Rama VII clearly reckoned that Siam's old tradition of maintaining concubines and multiple wives was not consistent with the ways of the newly industrialised nations of south-east Asia, and Siam wanted to be one of these.

The 1934 ruling against having multiple wives did not extend to a ban on prostitution, which remained legal at this time. Because of the new law prostitution started to become more popular, or at least more openly visible. The deployment of Thai troops in the north of the country at the beginning of the Second World War and an occupying army of Japanese troops in 1941 saw the first big boom in the industry. Thailand's participation in this war was ambiguous and half-hearted throughout. The Japanese had gained control Malaya and Burma, so the government of the time complied with Japan and theoretically declared war on the Allies. But this move had little popular support and the Thai ambassador in Washington refused to deliver the ultimatum. The country remained under occupation but effectively neutral. Some 300,000 Japanese soldiers were deployed in Thailand, or Siam, as it still then was. In fact it was during this occupation, and perhaps because of it, that the new name for the country, 'Thailand', meaning 'Land of the Free' was first coined and officially adopted later in 1949.

The 300,000 Japanese troops in Bangkok and the 30,000 British and Indian troops which came after them when the war was over in 1945 combined with the local population of Thais and Chinese to fill Bangkok's eighty-five cabaret clubs. These were all open air and they all had a resident dance troupe, a large dance floor and orchestras of various kinds . . . And, as a post-war American delegate to the country put it, 'scores, even hundreds, of peppermint-sipping dance partners'.[2] More colonial in character than the cramped modern bars with their loud rock music, pool tables, television screens and bar girls, perhaps, but these clusters of night spots were their original 1940s' precursors.

A law was passed in the 1950s forbidding prostitution. It may as well not have been, for all the effect it had. The business was by now far too important to the economy. A decade later, in the late 1960s and early 1970s, it was to get its second big boost. Again, war was the reason, this time the so-called 'Vietnam War' declared by American against the Communist regimes of Indo-China. Bangkok was a favourite spot for 'R and R' (rest and recreation) for American GIs, then soon afterwards Pattaya, a coastal resort with good beaches 150 kilometres south-east of the capital city. The (in Thailand's terms) seemingly incredible wealth of the Americans together with their insatiable recreational appetites lifted the small fishing village of Pattaya out of its slumber and into the throbbing entertainment machine it is today. The Chinese-owned Patpong area of Bangkok also became a Mecca of hedonism as the dollars poured in.

The next two decades witnessed one of the most extraordinary contradictions that are so characteristic of the country. Prostitution was illegal but this was a period not only of explosive economic growth but also of shameless promotion of the country as a destination for sex tourists. A survey carried out by Mahidol University in 1980 showed that the number of bars, clubs and disguised brothels in Bangkok alone had grown to 977. The number of girls in the city involved in prostitution, including free-lancers, was reckoned to be about 200,000. Up until the late 1980s tours were on offer, notably in Japan and Germany with the specific purpose of 'sex shopping'. Japanese companies openly provided annual sex tours for their employees to Thailand, Korea or the Philippines, flights and accommodation included. By the mid 1980s one out of two visitors to Thailand was an unaccompanied male.[3] In the late 1980s feminists took exception to this practice and the organisers of such tours came in for much vilification in public media. Company executives arriving back home from such trips would find themselves harangued at airports.

This vociferous campaign had two consequences. The first, predictably, was that the tour operators simply adopted a lower public profile. The tours still went on but involved less blatant publicity and smaller parties of tourists. Japanese men were notoriously the main patrons of the sex industry and the second response was to bring the industry to them. So in the late 1980s a network of organisations sprang up by which thousands of Thai and Filipino prostitutes were trafficked to Japan. The legacy of the Japanese presence is still very much in evidence in Bangkok where there are still bars with entrances displaying the message 'Japanese Only'.

The Internal Industry

For better or worse – whatever moral position one takes – it cannot be denied that sex tourism has become a major industry in Thailand. But tourism is only the tip of the industry's iceberg. According to Dr Suteera Thomson, president of Thailand's Society for the Promotion of Women, and an authority in this area,

> The link is small in terms of the number of foreign tourists patronising prostitution. If we base our rough calculation on the number of sex workers, the number of customers per day and the number of foreign tourists in Thailand, my observation is that the majority of the customers patronising prostitutes are Thai men; only a fraction are foreign tourists.

Estimates have it that the tourist sex industry represents only about 5 per cent of contact between customer and sex worker in Thailand, and that 95 per cent, or thereabouts, is confined to Thai nationals.[4]

The tourist side of the business is flagrant. The many thousands of bars and massage parlours compete with one another for the attention of passing tourists with their garish neon signs, beckoning girls and touts on the street waving faded photographs. The internal sex industry, on the other hand, is altogether a much more private, Thai, and sometimes sinister affair, going on behind the closed doors of anonymous houses and buildings. According to travel writer Alistair Shearer, 'It is run by locals, including a large number of Chinese, and every Thai town has in addition to the establishments geared to tourists, its local whorehouse, the vast majority of which have never been visited by a single *farang*.'[5] The origins of these places can be traced back to the mid nineteenth century when Chinese immigrants established a brothel area in Bangkok's Sampeng Lane. For a time all the prostitutes were Chinese. When Thai women arrived on the scene later this century they usually took Chinese names. Nowadays the prostitutes come from many different ethnic backgrounds, including, over recent years, women from Russia.[6]

Before the beginnings of prostitution different sexual outlets existed for married and unmarried men. There was nothing in the moral code of the times to prevent those men who could afford it from having mistresses, or 'minor wives' (*mia noi*). Wealthy men kept at least one *sohphenii* – a Sanskrit term for exceptionally beautiful women who had undergone a protracted period of training in the arts of entertaining men – along the same lines as the *Geisha* of Japan. And one might speculate that, with their likely ancient history, *kathoey* predated prostitutes as a legitimate sexual outlet for the less well off.

Researcher and lecturer at Birmingham University, Louise Brown, has published a fascinating exposé of the trafficking of prostitutes in Asia and south-east Asia. Her book, entitled *Sex Slaves*, published by Virago in 2000, lays bare the astonishing scale of this practice and the complex network of agents, traffickers and the '*mamasan*' who run and often own the brothels upon which this industry depends. In some of the poorest regions such as Nepal and Myanmar (Burma), girls are taken from their families, even sold by them, and transported to a brothel. This happens in northern Thailand too but here the recruitment of girls is largely an open matter. Louise Brown writes,

> Here trafficking is not really the best description to apply to the recruitment and transportation of girls for prostitution. Rural-urban migration aided by a network of employment agents is a far better description of the trade. Coercion is rarely employed and girls are not deceived . . . Agents work openly in the villages and compete with one another over the deals they can offer . . . In parts of Thailand, as well as other countries like Vietnam, the family's attention is not focused on safeguarding their daughter from prostitution. On the contrary, the critical issue is the kind of brothel she will work in. The measure of concern is the reputation of the brothel and the reliability of the agent who takes her there.[7]

Some girls are trafficked on to work in brothels in other countries such as Singapore, South Korea or Japan.

Brown provides evidence that in some of the poorer countries girls are groomed to be sold as prostitutes from an early age. However, this is not the case in Thailand. In contrast to the free-wheeling attitude of the authorities towards the adult sex trade, Thailand has one of the most active anti child abuse programmes in south-east Asia. The age of consent in Thailand is fifteen and attempts to stamp out the exploitation of children under this age – a collaborative initiative with the U.K. and other Western countries – has met with considerable success. Posters publicising the campaign abound in even the seediest establishments in Bangkok and Pattaya. Notices on the doors of the go-go bars of the 'Soi Cowboy' area of Bangkok where expatriates like to gather display the sign 'All Models are Over 21'. A dubious claim perhaps but the level of vigilance by the police is high and children are not in evidence at these places.

The lives of those *kathoey* who become prostitutes follow a similar course to those of the women who do so. Their numbers are smaller of course and it could be said that they enter the profession with more of a degree of choice and less as a result of coercion from their families or from 'agents'. If there is any coercion this takes the form of economic necessity and the temptation to earn in a year or two more than their farming families earn in a lifetime. They are rarely pushed into the sex industry, but often they are not exactly discouraged, especially when the money starts to flow back home.

It is well known that Thai prostitutes have found their way to many European capital cities. So too have *kathoey* prostitutes, although, again, by comparison, their numbers are small. Amsterdam is a favourite destination for them and they have an established presence there.

Another Contradiction?

It is often said that Thailand is a country full of apparent paradoxes and contradictions to the Western observer. One of the most puzzling is the seeming coexistence of a liberal (some might say excessively liberal) lack of censorship over matters of sex with a strong ethic of family ties and fidelity.

After the end of the Second World War in 1945, the American government of the time regarded the Communist elements in some of Thailand's neighbouring countries as a potential threat. It set about establishing more than diplomatic relations with Thailand by dispatching a group of delegates whose aim was to establish an American presence in the country and who came armed with the offer of economic aid. Among these was one J. Orgibet from the Office of Strategic Services (OSS) as this organisation was known before it became the CIA. Orgibet later became a journalist and broadcaster in Thailand and relates some of his experiences in a book entitled, *From Siam to Thailand. Backdrop to the Land of Smiles.* He sums up traditional Thai hospitality in the following passage,

In up-country Siam in the old days an honoured guest in a home was offered the best that house had to offer, be it a farmer's shack or Governor's mansion. So that an honoured guest's every comfort was provided, you should not have to sleep alone. Therefore, the best the house had to offer was yours. The best may be a sister, No. 2 wife, aunt, niece, even daughter, but never the No. 1 wife.

Providing a distinguished male visitor with female company has long been an essential part of Thai hospitality, as the records of numerous travel writers attest, as far back as the Dutch merchants visiting Pattani in 1604. The men of Siam have historically enjoyed a licence to stray beyond the marital bed and this habit is by no means defunct. In contemporary Thailand it is reckoned that most Thai men are regular customers of prostitutes. The sanctity of marriage is protected (at least on the face of it) in the inviolable status of the No. 1 wife and in the lifetime obligations of the younger family members to their elders.

'Prostitutes Are Better Than Lovers' is the title of a recent study of women's attitudes to the promiscuity of the men of modern Thailand.[8] The authors comment on the general acceptability of single Thai men visiting prostitutes:

> . . . Most Thais, whether men or women, hold relatively tolerant attitudes regarding sex with prostitutes in the case of single men. The focus group discussions (the data of this study) of both men and women indicate that visiting prostitutes is judged as both normal (*thammada*) and appropriate (*mor-som*) behaviour for single men given the perceived strong natural male sexual urge.

In respect of married couples the findings of the study '. . . in dicate that wives are generally more concerned about the consequences of extra-marital non-commercial sexual relations than commercial sexual relations'. In other words visits to a prostitute are seen as the lesser of two evils and therefore tend to be tolerated.

'*Katheoey* are better than *puying* (girls)' is a comment I have heard made by some Thai men. Anthropologist Peter Jackson and others have suggested that *kathoey* prostitutes historically may have been favoured over girls as a less problematic sexual outlet for unmarried males.[9]

Echoes of Siam's patriarchal past still resound.

Chapter 9
Transgender in Other Cultures

Anthropologists who have made studies of 'primitive', or pre-civilised cultures have often commented on a transgendered (male-to-female) minority who appear to be, and to have been for a long while, an integral part of one of these cultures. And, like *kathoey*, these 'third sex' people enjoy an acknowledged and legitimate position in the societies of which they are part. They have been found in quite diverse parts of the globe, and their accreditation within the broader frame is encrypted in the very terms for them that have currency in these societies; for example, the *berdache* of old north and central America,[1] the *hijra* of India,[2] the *waria* and *bissu* of Indonesia,[3] the *mahu* and *fa'afafines* of Polynesia and Samoa[4], the *asog* of the Philippines,[5] and the *ne'uchica* of eastern Siberia.[6]

In the much studied North American Indians some kind of reference to people who were not readily classifiable either as men or women is documented from the sixteenth century on wards in nearly 150 North American tribes. What similarities and parallels, if any, are there in the way these people behave and are treated by the others of their community?

Certainly, many of these groups presented a surprise to the European explorers who saw them for the first time. The more pious amongst them felt threatened as they confronted something which the Christian model of woman and man did not equip them to understand. Their reaction was, perhaps predictably, one of horror of these 'abominable' and 'unspeakable' practices.[7] Such a reaction is typified in an observation about the first European arrivals in Polynesia in the late eighteenth and early nineteenth centuries: 'Evangelical missionaries had little doubt that Satan, adversary of God and man, reigned as absolute sovereign over the South Sea Islands.'[8]

The reactions of the less refined travellers of the time was not so censorious if this comment of historian Niko Besnier's is to be believed: 'Recurrent in early testimonies is the theme of the horny European sailor mistaking a Polynesian gender-liminal (third sex) person for a woman.' He alludes to stories of sailors going with 'girls' (parentheses his) who were dancers at festivals.[9]

Comparisons between very different cultures in very different parts of the world of course need to be approached with caution. There is no *a priori* reason to assume that the various different transgendered groups that have been discovered in these cultures fulfil a similar role, or enjoy a similar context, within the broader social framework of which they are part. In Thailand itself two distinct species of *kathoey* can be identified: the traditional *kathoey* of old rural Siam, especially the undeveloped north and north-east, and the modern day *kathoey* cabaret performer of the tourist cities. The latter are a relatively recent invention, only appearing in significant numbers when the first commercial cabaret shows sprang up in the town of Pattaya in the 1960s and 1970s. This was the time when Pattaya was being transformed out of all recognition from the small fishing village it used to be into the garish tourist attraction it is today. It was not until flocks of young hopefuls, such as Lek, hearing tales of big money, made their way from the villages to the glitzy new venues that this category of *kathoey* as high profile entertainer of tourists emerged, many of the old traditions soon to be lost in the frenetic atmosphere of opportunity and financial gain. There would appear to be no direct equivalent to this in other countries, certainly nothing on this scale. Even if there were, any comparisons with the older traditions would be of limited value because this particular version of transgendered person must be seen as a modern product of the powerful combined forces of economic deprivation, family obligation and commercial opportunism.

However, not to compare the traditions of these different groups in their different countries would be as bad a mistake as to start with the preconception that they all occupy the same structural and functional space in the wider frame. At least on the face of it, a reading of the existing literature does appear to reveal some interesting correspondences, even across groups in very different geographical locations. To start with, it strongly suggests that indigenous transgendered groups are normal to 'primitive' communities. This word is taken to mean Animist cultures with ancient roots that have not yet been taken over by, or assimilated into, the so-called civilising influence of a larger-scale religious or political order.

Remnants of Animism are few and far between in the modern world, so much of this research draws on historical documents and the reports of anthropologists writing at the turn of the nineteenth and beginning of the twentieth centuries. One of the spin-offs from feminist and women's studies has been an increased interest over the last ten to fifteen years in what has become known as 'gender studies' among academics in American and European universities, with the result that a number of scholarly papers are available that review and evaluate these older sources.[10]

Some classic studies of North American Indians were made by anthropologists in the first half of the twentieth century. Third-gender individuals were seen in numerous tribes and were dubbed *berdache* by the writers of the time – a term now unfashionable amongst scholars as it is considered somewhat derogatory in connotation. Modern writers prefer the more pedantic terms 'third spirit', and 'woman-man'. Third-sex people appear to have been widespread and have been described in cultures as geographically diverse as the Arctic, Mississippi, Mexico and what is now California. Sabine Lang, summarising the received knowledge, writes,

It seems, however, that one generalising statement that can be rightfully made is that most of those widely different cultures at least traditionally recognised more than two genders . . . In a number of these tribes women-men (the unstigmatised modern term, preferred to *berdache*) are medicine people of one kind or another. In some tribes they will be viewed as being eligible for such a position because of their special gender status.[11]

Similar attributions of spiritual potency attaching to trans-gendered males have been made in even more diverse parts of the northern hemisphere. Marjorie Balzer[12] describes such a link in the Animist communities in north-east Siberia. She quotes the remarks of an early researcher, Borgaras, writing in 1909 about a young shaman named Tilu'wgi:

> Tilu'wgi's face, encircled with braids of thick hair, arranged after the manner of a Chukchee woman, looked very different from masculine faces. It was something like a female tragic mask, fitted to the body of a giantess of a race different from our own. All the ways of this strange creature were decidedly feminine.

According to the *Oxford English Dictionary* the word 'shaman' originated in Siberia, although it is commonly applied to mediums in any culture that practises Animist-style spirit healing. In Siberia gender ambiguity is associated with mysterious sexual energy from which it is believed derives a special potency to conjure and command spirits in order to achieve a desired result; for example, a cure or fertility. The supernatural spirits in turn guide gender transformations and are believed to have a close tie with their wards, sometimes marrying them in special spirit-human unions. Because these spirits are believed to be especially powerful and potentially vengeful, the meek and effeminate men with whom they are in league are feared. From this mutually fuelling relationship between spirit and transformed shaman comes his attributed power to cure, or otherwise alter, earthly situations.

Balzer regards the bear festivals as, 'a community-wide spiritual healing, growing and socialising drama . . . an occasion for both reinforcement of human-spirit relations and social critique'. Men took on women's parts just for that event. In the more intimate environment of the séance, gender transformation of the presiding shaman was a matter of

alien did these seem to their own civilisations and the Catholic beliefs upon which these were founded. To them the rituals of spirit worship represented straightforward sin and sinners were to be called to account and punished. The Christian missionaries of the nineteenth and early twentieth centuries appear to have taken a somewhat softer line. Their faith, of course, did not allow them to condone Animist practices, but these tended to be explained as the products of ignorance and 'freakishness' rather than the work of the devil. Their practitioners were more to be pitied and educated rather than feared and put to the sword.

India's Hijra

In her book entitled *Neither Man nor Woman*,[17] Serena Nanda gives a fascinating account of the *hijras* of India. *Hijras* are India's third sex. They are a religious community of males (ostensibly) who dress and act like women and who worship the goddess Mata, one of the many versions of the mother Goddess worshipped throughout India. In connection with this worship the person becomes a true *hijra* by undergoing castration usually at the hands of another more senior member of the community (the procedure is illegal in India and takes place in private houses without the administration of an anaesthetic). *Hijras* have a traditional role in India as performers at marriages and at homes where a male child has just been born. The birth of a son is considered the most important event for an Indian family. *Hijras* attend the home, ritually bless the newborn child and entertain the family with music, dance and song. A typical group of performers consists of two musicians, five dancers and a senior guru who directs the proceedings. These celebrations are a source of much laughter and fun. In return for their performances the *hijra* receive money and gifts from the family.

In a sense *hijras* are one of the most 'successful' of the traditional transgender communities in Asia in terms of their sitting comfortably with, and complementing, the prevailing religion of the day. *Hijras* are mostly, but not exclusively Hindu. A minority are Muslim. They tend to live together in

communities, or 'houses', within which there is a clear structure of roles and a family-style supportive framework.

Both *hijra* and *kathoey* traditionally specialise as professional performers and entertainers. The cultural space occupied by *kathoey* would thus seem to be more like that of the
hijra of India than the *berdache* of north America and those
other transgendered groups that have been described in
countries where there is a close correspondence between
shamanism and gender ambiguity. Indeed, the entertainment
that *hijra* and *kathoey* offer their audiences would seem to be
quite similar in style, if not in content. They both have the
reputation of being outrageous in their performance and typically of crossing normal boundaries of etiquette and
respectability. There are parallels too in the conventions of
performance – *hijra* also rely on receiving 'tips' at such
events. Nanda writes:

> Like the performance at birth, the typical performing
> group at a marriage in a middle-class family consists of
> five to nine *hijras*; most of them dance, one plays the
> drums, and one plays the harmonium . . . The more elab-
> orate performances . . . occur in upper-middle-class fami-
> lies, and the money and gifts (similar to those given at a
> birth) demanded by the *hijras* correspond to that status. It
> is expected that elder members of the audience will bless
> the groom by circling his head with rupee notes and this
> money is also collected by the *hijras* (p.4).

There are yet further similarities between the two groups.
Children typically decide they want to become *hijras* or
kathoey at an early age. A novice will have a mentor. In the
case of *kathoey* this is an 'older sister', for *hijra* it is the more
formal 'guru'. Many *hijras* at some stage in their lives earn a
living as prostitutes. A full *hijra* is one with emasculated genitalia, just as to be considered a full *kathoey* one must have
had 'the operation'. The majority of *hijra* are Hindu, and
Hindu myths and legends, like those of Buddhism, a deriva-
tive of Hinduism, contain numerous references to androgynous people and gods. *Hijra* are a recognised institution of

Indian society and like *kathoey* are considered in the broader culture with the same paradoxical mix of respect and disdain. The everyday habits of the two groups are similar; they dress and deport themselves with exaggerated, even aggressive, femininity, they almost all smoke and they are not shy of responding to criticism with a loud and a sharp tongue which makes them to some extent feared. Individuals in both groups commonly express the melancholic desire to give birth to children.

Polynesia is another part of the world in which transgender would seem to be associated with open festivities, dancing and public performance rather than the more private rituals of spirit healing. Besnier comments on the 'striking association' of gender ambiguity with satire and the burlesque in these islands.[18] Like *kathoey* and *hijra*, the heritage of these folk as entertainers appears to have survived into the modern world.

Conclusion

Transgendered groups of people have been described by anthropologists as indigenous to Animist cultures in many different parts of the world.

Men posing and dressing as women and vice-versa are not of course something that is unique to these ancient Animist cultures. There have been reports of cross-dressing in Christian times, Henri III of France and Joan of Arc being two famous examples. Some less famous cases have been documented by Dutch social historians Rudolf Dekker and Lotte van der Pol, throughout Europe from the sixteenth through to the nineteenth centuries.[19] Many of these are the stories of women who dressed themselves as men for a specific purpose – so as to join the army or sign on board for ships headed to the Dutch West Indies in order to make their fortunes there.

These examples are relatively few and far between and the motivation behind cross-dressing was either pragmatic (e.g. wanting to join the armed forces), or just plain eccentric. There is nothing in the Judaeo-Christian world remotely comparable to the groups described above; sets of people apparently born boys who at an early age express a wish to act and dress as girls; sets of people, moreover, who are acknowledged in the broader community as a third type of gender in their own right, independent of men and women, and who comprise an integral part of that community and as such are accorded recognition and even status.

One thing at least appears clear from these anthropologists' reports. Those cultures that have traditionally accepted, and to some extent embraced, a minority group among them of individuals who are neither men nor women are those rooted in Animist traditions. Where Animist traditions persist in their ancient forms, so it appears does the tradition of gender ambiguity and a third sex. When Animist practices have had to adapt to, or merge with, waves of more legislative philosophies and ideologies as these have swept in, the third sex has also had to adapt, or go underground.

If Animist beliefs and spirit worship together with their rituals and superstitions were anathema and loathsome to the colonising Christians, such practices did not pose the same threat to the Hindu and Buddhist priesthood when these religions spread through south and south-east Asia. Much of the old Animist mythology became incorporated into the legends and imagery of these religions. Indeed, it is fair to say that Hinduism and Buddhism to some extent remoulded their ideologies and doctrines so as to avoid conflict with the old pre-canonical traditions which were, of course, very widespread. The assimilation of many of the old ideas into the new doctrines helped to insure the smooth passage of the latter.

As well as similarities, comparisons between different transgendered categories in different parts of the world also reveal differences and contrasts. *Kathoey* seem to have more in common with those groups concerned with public performance than those practising witchcraft and spirit healing. With their exhibitionist femininity, their preoccupation with physical appearance and their theatrical leanings they appear more like the *hijra* of India, the *mahu* of Polynesia and the *fa'afafines* of Samoa than the north American *berdache* and the shamans of eastern Siberia. Unlike these last two groups their speciality would seem to have been that of entertainer rather than spirit healer or shaman.[20]

And again, like *hijra*, in the course of history *kathoey* struck up a quasi-partnership with the formal religions when these arrived on the scene (Hinduism in India, Buddhism in Siam). Both complemented the teachings and liturgies of the monks by providing light-hearted secular entertainment to mark auspicious or festive occasions. *Hijra* and *kathoey* were the purveyors of fun after the priests had delivered their sermons and blessings.

Similarities in what happened to Animist communities when their homeland was over-run by a colonial power are readily apparent. The highly doctrinaire, politically driven, invader must, by definition, in order to keep intact his own system of beliefs, reject practices that are violently at odds with his construction of the world. The tight canons of medieval Christianity did not include provision for the recognition of other religions, especially Godless ones, and they certainly did not recognise any variation from the male-female dichotomy of the story of the Creation. The icon of the beautiful feminised male with mysterious powers over nature must have presented about the most extreme opposite to the orthodoxy of the day it is possible to conceive. It had, as a matter of urgency, to be crushed and replaced by the legend of the machismo male, ultimately crystallised in the Hollywood stereotype of the tough guy with a raging heterosexual appetite; the John Wayne of the prairie, the *banditos* of Mexico. On the other side of the world the Siberia of the 1920s saw a similar transformation. The transgender shamans of the north-east were an abomination to the new Communist regime. This time it was the state that imposed its stamp on the definition of gender.

There was, of course, no conceivable basis for any kind of discourse between the Animists and their new Christian masters. They were just too metaphysically removed from one another. The easiest way for the invaders to deal with the problem was to stamp out these phenomena that they could never hope to understand. They had the muscle to do so, as well as the motivation. The softer methods of the missionaries

were nevertheless reputedly very effective in enforcing 'con-
formity of the population into . . . a two sex, two gender
model'.[21] In many cases their only hope of survival was for
third-sex people to assume a low profile. This baleful sce-
nario is nicely summed up in the title of a book by Ramon
Gutiérrez concerned with events in New Mexico from 1500
to 1846 – *When Jesus Came The Corn Mothers Went
Away*.[22] The irony is, of course, that it was not Jesus – cham-
pion of minorities and the underdog – but the heavyweight
powers of the day who found Animism and its associated
practices so indigestible.

Chapter 10
Daeng's Story

Daeng was twenty-five when I first met her at a small cabaret theatre in Chiang Mai. At the time of writing this book she was twenty-seven and I had known her for two and a bit years. As a child she had had the boy's name Akorn. Daeng insists that her former self, Akorn, knew he wanted to be *kathoey* from the age of four. Her old school friends, Lek and Malee (formerly Lek and Manat) confirmed to me that this was indeed the case. For them the realisation came later, when they had turned ten years of age.

Saowanee, Akorn's senior at the Secondary School, agreed to become his elder 'sister' when he was thirteen and they have continued to be good friends to this day. It was Akorn's teenage fancy to take on the name 'Champagne', but Saowanee came down against this idea and a year later, at the age of fourteen, Akorn became 'Daeng'. This can be the name of a boy or a girl and it means 'red'.

Throughout her years as a senior at Rama V School Daeng grew more and more confident in her chosen role as *kathoey*. Saowanee had proved an excellent 'sister'. She took considerable pleasure in teaching Daeng the artifices of femininity – dress, hair, shoes, make-up, movement and mannerisms. She explained the workings of the various oestrogen-based oral hormones on offer. These were available to anyone, even school kids, over-the-counter, and Saowanee had recommended that Daeng start taking the pills straightaway at the age of fourteen. The earlier a child started, the greater the long-term effect the hormones had on bone structure, muscle mass, skin character and breast development. Daeng's pills contained a mix of oestrogen, progesterone and anti-androgens.[1] The oestrogen content was three to four times that produced naturally in females. According to the doctor this was safe, since the target organs for side-effects of oestrogen overproduction were typically the female organs.

Daeng was a quick learner and, by her final year, her appearance and demeanour were not so much those of a girl but of a confident young woman. The physical effects of the hormones had kicked in and at seventeen she had developed small but distinctive breasts helped along by a padded bra.

The staff at the school had no difficulty accepting the transformation. They had seen it before and were impressed by this one's beauty and iron-like determination. Within the school walls, and to a certain extent outside them, the matter was not considered taboo and was openly discussed, especially among the female staff who were quick to comment with enthusiasm on a new dress or hair style. '*Suey mark*', meaning 'very beautiful', a chorus of women teachers would say when Daeng appeared in a new dress or with a new hair style (the openly expressed admiration amongst Thai women for a *kathoey's* beauty and detailed comments about hair, make-up and body was something I was to witness many times during the course of my visits to Thailand). Neither was there a problem with her parents. Her father, if at first a shade disappointed – Daeng would have been the only son and this carries prestige in a Thai family – was careful not to show it. They were sensitive folk who belonged to Thailand's relatively new middle class. Her mother had accurately and privately read the situation when Daeng was six years old. All Daeng's playmates at this age were girls and a preference for wearing a skirt rather than the regulation school shorts had made itself awkwardly apparent. She had said nothing on the several occasions when she discovered her make-up was not as she had left it.

At nineteen Daeng left the school for Chiang Mai University to study Philosophy and Comparative Religions. This was a departure from her original plan which was to study Dance and Theatre. In her later years at the school she had become intellectually curious and had changed her mind. Her father backed the decision, pointing out that she was bound to become involved with a dance group in any case, plus she was set on a career in dance, so why not spread her wings while she has the chance? Within a week she had absorbed the more liberal university regime, made new friends and felt herself to be popular and happy.

In the vacation after her first year at CMU, Daeng acquired breasts. At her father's insistence, and considerable expense, this was done in Singapore at a private clinic which specialises in cosmetic and so-called sex reassignment surgery (SRS). The operation is a reasonably straightforward one, consisting of silicone or collagen implants, but there can be serious, even potentially fatal, complications seven or eight years on if it is not done properly, since silicone can pass into the bloodstream and lungs.

Rosepaper

Daeng returned to her second year at CMU in good spirits, extremely proud of her new shape. She was determined to have full SRS as soon as she could afford it.

This was to prove an eventful time for the *kathoey* dance group at the university called Rosepaper. Daeng had joined the group as a general assistant and props manager in her first year. In her second year she could perform with them, and by her third and final years she had become assistant and stand-in for the principal choreographer who was a post-graduate student of dance and movement.

The group was popular with the other students and had for many years staged performances for them on the university campus. This they continued to do, but, in addition, an enterprising member of the group had negotiated the hire of a large room above a bar just outside the west gate of the university campus on the Doi Suthep Road. This they had converted to a small theatre with tables and chairs and a bar, and had opened it up to the public under the name 'Fascination'. Two shows were performed most evenings and a publicity machine of sorts ensured that they usually had an audience of some kind, whose size varied from two people to maybe a block booking of forty or fifty tourists from Japan or Korea. There was no admission charge, but drinks were at a premium at 200 baht, or £3 a round.

For a while, and throughout Daeng's student years, the venue did not exactly flourish as a commercial venture but it just about made ends meet and supplied a hotbed of talent and creativity. Performing daily at the venue, the students regarded themselves, rightly, as professionals and were prepared to put in any amount of energy and rehearsal time in order to present polished, professional shows. This indeed they did and they received warm notices in the press and a certain reputation in the town and with some of the local tour operators.

The initiative was eventually to founder, probably because the little venue was in a somewhat obscure location some four kilometres from the centre of town. Daeng was lucky enough to be part of the group when its work was at its most intense and its artistic standards at their highest. She fuelled these, spending every minute of her non-curriculum time working for the group, and in her fourth and final year, teaching many types of skill and helping devise new forms and routines. But, alas, audiences were too patchy for it to be able to meet its overheads, so after only a few years the venue was forced to close.[2]

The World

Daeng graduated from CMU with a middle grade. Unlike her friend Lek she had a clear-sighted vision of her first career move. She applied for an audition at Thailand's most glitzy and hitech cabaret – Alcazar in the coastal resort of Pattaya. Originally a small fishing village some 150 kilometres south of the capital, unregulated development beginning in the 1960s saw the place transform beyond recognition into the Mecca for tourists, with its frenetic night life, that it now is. Alcazar, bang in the centre of the town, is a highly successful commercial theatre seating 1,500. A cast of some sixty dancers, *kathoey* and boys, perform daily to large audiences of Japanese, Chinese and Europeans shipped in, in convoys of coaches. A visit to one of these shows is built in to their travel itinerary, much in the same way as a visit to a temple or the floating market. Shows are continually changed and refreshed, so the future of these profitable venues is virtually guaranteed: a far cry from Rosepaper's tiny hand-to-mouth enterprise.

Daeng had set her sights high and the sense of disappointment she felt when she failed the audition was new to her. There were two vacancies for dancers. All her friends, as well as the other contestants, had firmly expected her to fill one of these. She had delivered what she knew was a good performance at the audition and no explanation was given as to why she had not been accepted. Members of the cast consoled her by saying that such things were by no means uncommon in show business and can often be put down to a whim on the part of the manager/owner. Her more intimate friends pointed out that many of the dancers at Alcazar had undergone full SRS plus a spectrum of other cosmetic touches such as hip filling and facial enhancements.

Undeterred, Daeng applied for an audition at the somewhat less prestigious but equally successful theatre, Simon Cabaret on beautiful Phuket island. This time she was accepted and at twenty-two a new chapter in her life was about to begin.

The first thing she found out was that life on the payroll of one of these establishments was a lot tougher than she had imagined. Her childhood, school and university years had been little short of ideal – a clever and talented child with understanding parents and an absence of poverty and want. This was a rare combination where she came from. She looked back on her time with Rosepaper and Fascination as golden days. Now she was encountering a harder, altogether less predictable, world. Dancers were required to perform two or three shows a day seven days a week. When she started her new job there was no mention at all of any time off. In addition, most afternoons were given over to rehearsing new routines in line with the theatre's policy to have the show continually changing and evolving. After rehearsal it was time to make up for the first show. Pay was hardly generous, on a scale from 6,000 baht a month (£100) for the juniors to 10,000 baht for the principal dancers.

If this sounds like bonded labour, let it be said that the

majority of the dancers, almost all of whom came from poor families, considered themselves much more fortunate than their peers who were in factory jobs or who had joined the ranks of Bangkok's hostesses and 'bar girls'. They were probably not any better off financially but they enjoyed a certain status within the Thai community as professional performers. Despite the long hours, little time off and subsistence pay, their employment was reasonably secure, as long as they kept up a good standard of performance.

None of the performers who worked at the cabaret could afford a flat of their own. Daeng had the offer of living with two others in an apartment with one bedroom, bathroom and balcony. This she accepted

Apart from the physical demands of dancing three shows every day there were other surprises. The monthly salary was hardly enough to live on and it was expected of a performer to make this up to meet her needs by posing for tourists' cameras and camcorders after each show. So the dancers would line up in costume and compete for 'tips' to pose for photographs. The standard tip was 20 baht (30p), but the trick was to spot the wealthier tourist and try for a larger sum.

The other, more lucrative, way for a dancer to raise her income above the level of bare subsistence was to arrange an assignation with a customer after the last show. Daeng had heard that this went on but was unprepared for the extent of the practice and the apparent casualness with which it was treated. One of her flat-mates, Sai, would regularly return home at 3 or 4 in the morning or not at all. No secret was made of this to the newcomer, and Sai was happy to discuss the protocol and the payment that could be expected. The latter depended on your bargaining power and could be anything from 500 to 2,000 baht (60 baht to the pound). It was possible to double or treble the monthly income of 6,000 baht in this way. Many, but not all of the girls, did this. Not surprisingly those who made themselves most available were the ones from the poorest families.

Daeng's attitude to this practice was at first disdainful, but before long she realised the unfairness of this stance. She was receiving a regular allowance from her father (which she had kept to herself). For most of the others the flow of money was in the other direction: any surplus cash was sent back to their families. The poor families of the north and north-east were more than happy to receive this regular support and did not ask too many questions about where the money came from. The donors had the double satisfaction of not only being able to help their families, but also gaining spiritual or kammic credit in the Buddhist scheme of things.

So Daeng settled into her new life uneasily. She was clearly the belle of the troupe if this could be measured by the amount she was receiving in tips for photographs. This, in a sense, made her situation even more awkward. The fact she did not appear to want for money led to a certain resentment among some of the others, though not among her flat-mates with whom she had fast become close friends. Pride and mounting guilt about her protected position in the community soon led her to write to her father, lying about her salary, saying she had received a rise and that she no longer needed a supplement from the family coffers. She said she was now earning enough to be self-sufficient. This move served to salve her conscience for a time but she was to have second thoughts about its wisdom when in the following weeks she found herself struggling to pay the bills and having to do without the extras such as new clothes to which she had grown accustomed.

Five months into her new job and she still felt different from the others, even without the support from her father. She was performing well at the theatre, but so far had not had the offer of a more senior role and better pay that she had been hoping for and felt she deserved. She was not by nature an extravagant person, but she was not accustomed to the relative poverty she was now having to endure.

Eric

Until she met Eric, Daeng had not had a relationship of any kind. Eric was from Switzerland and thirty-two years old. He was her first. He was on holiday in Phuket and had been to see the cabaret three times in one week. Third time round he asked Daeng out for a meal and Daeng found herself accepting. The others were sometimes taken out, so why not her? This was the beginning. He was bespectacled, polite, a little shy, and to Daeng the archetype of European chivalry. Thereafter he began to date her on a regular basis, taking her to restaurants, jazz clubs and discos. Thais seen with *farang* are generally regarded with disdain by professional-class Thais. Respectable middle-class Daeng manufactured the justification that it is not uncommon for a Thai to marry a European and for them to live together and be respected members of the community. This, of course, was twisted thinking in the extreme. Thai law does not permit *kathoey* to change their gender from that assigned to them at birth. Their passports and identity cards must therefore bear the title 'Mr' and they are stuck with this – a fact bitterly resented throughout the community. They cannot marry men in Thailand. A few cases are talked about where individuals have managed to obtain visas and have emigrated to a European country where they can under modern law change their legal status to that of a woman and get married. There was even talk of some successful and happy partnerships.

A month from their first date proved their relationship was other than casual. Eric renewed his visa and extended his stay in Thailand. He was single and his job was to edit scripts for television documentaries. Modern communication technology meant that he could carry on this work in Thailand more or less as effectively as in Switzerland and his producer had agreed he could extend his stay for a further month.

As their relationship continued and deepened Eric ventured to suggest Daeng might consider going back with him to Switzerland, initially perhaps for a 'trial' period. He would assist with her visa application at the Swiss embassy in Bangkok and would of course pay the air fare.

For Daeng the prospect of leaving her homeland, her family and friends at this stage in her life was a non-starter. As is the case for most *kathoey* she was steeped in the Buddhist tradition and a regular worshipper at the temple. Rarely would she pass even the smallest shrine without stopping to show her devotion with a *wai* or a longer prayer. She had nothing against other religions but could not conceive what it would be like to live in a Christian or Buddha-less country.

So Eric stayed on in Thailand for a further six months, with the help of a dubious visa that it was possible to purchase from a company in Bangkok run by a Swede that advertised itself as selling visas, visa extensions, work permits and marriage certificates to aliens. He rented an airy apartment close to the sea and Daeng moved in with him. For the time being her money worries were over.

SRS

Daeng continued to work with the same troupe of dancers. Many of these had already undergone full sex reassignment surgery (SRS), which consists of remodelling the existing male organs into an approximation of female ones. Much earlier in her life she knew that this is what she eventually wanted. Now it was starting to preoccupy her. She felt able to confide in Eric and they had many conversations about it. Eric would help with the cost and Daeng made enquiries about the reputations of the clinics and doctors who specialised in this procedure. She did not want to ask her parents for money, but each time she telephoned home she was unable to prevent herself from broaching the subject to her mother. It soon became clear to everyone that in order to avert depression and a possible mental crisis some sort of a plan had to be laid down.

Some days off work were negotiated with her boss and the pair of them travelled to Chiang Mai with the dual aims of introducing Eric to Daeng's family and discussing the matter of her psychological need, which just recently had become pressing, to undergo full SRS.

It was agreed that regardless of expense the best clinic in Bangkok[3] should be consulted and that the family and Eric would jointly foot the bill. Daeng would need several weeks off work and this too would have to a paid for. Eric was no doubt pleasantly surprised, not to say relieved, to find his reception by Daeng's parents warm and cordial.

A year on Daeng had completed and recovered from the SRS and post-operative proceedings. She was fit and well, and now a full *kathoey* and very proud of it. She said the operation was painful and recovery slow, but the psychological liberation she felt was immeasurable. The longed for transformation was complete. She looked like a woman, acted like a woman and felt like a woman. She rejoined her dancing troupe feeling that, like many of the others, now she had gone through the final, ultimate test. At last she really felt she had *arrived* at her true destiny.

Eric had returned to Switzerland. They wrote and sent e-mails to each other for a time but this correspondence gradually dwindled, as each of them settled back into their own incommensurable cultures, lives and routines. So different was the world to which Eric had returned from the one he had known on Phuket island that the images of his seven months there were too fantastic to be sustained and it was not long before memory blurred and imagination failed.

Daeng had moved back into her old apartment with the same two friends. They threw her a party and told her that her new status as a full *kathoey* was bound to help her career.

Miss Tiffany

In the month of March the two big cabaret theatres in Pattaya, Alcazar and Tiffany, stage beauty contests. Hundreds of *kathoey* compete for the title 'Miss Alcazar' or 'Miss Tiffany'. Considerable media hype surrounds these events and the two venues make windfall profits. These contests had started to attract as much attention and coverage as the competition for the title 'Miss Thailand'. Indeed the previous year Miss Alcazar was widely billed in the press as outclassing the 'Miss Thailand' of that year. The winners of these contests enjoy publicity in the national press, on television and on the front covers of magazines, but surprisingly little money compared to that raked in by the venues and the promoters of such events.

Daeng's friends hatched the idea that she should enter one of these competitions. She took little persuading but insisted that before she appeared on the catwalk she should have some minor alterations to parts of her face. This is common practice not only among *kathoey* but also among professional female models of all nationalities. The simplest and least drastic method is the injection of small quantities of silicone in designated regions by a qualified practitioner. This requires neither a general anaesthetic nor a stay in hospital. A good beauty clinic was chosen and after two sessions her companions approved the result. The areas treated had to be massaged for several hours after the treatment with crushed ice bound in a cloth.

Daeng told me that she became uncomfortably aware at this time of a wave of envy from certain of the other performers. Everyone knew she would get through the first round to the final. What they were less prepared for was Daeng's winning the final and the title 'Miss Tiffany'. The usual flood of publicity followed the contests with air tickets and escorts to a top Bangkok photographic studio, press interviews and television appearances. Fame of a sort, and money changing hands. But her naïve ignorance of the world of media and the lack of guidance in the form of a manager or professional adviser meant that very little of this money ended up in the hands of the superstar herself.

Surprisingly she was not offered work at Tiffany's. She hated the town of Pattaya anyway and was pleased to return to her friends and the more modest, more intimate Simon cabaret in Phuket. But only for a while.

Needles and Glass

It was two years on from her earning the title 'Miss Tiffany' that I was to meet Daeng in the small theatre in Chiang Mai and come to know her and listen to her story. There was plenty of time for this to unfold as I was to have the good fortune to be invited to live in the family home.

The intervening years had not been happy ones. She told me how in Phuket when she was still working at Simon Cabaret she had her first real taste of the darker side of human nature. Towards the end of the show she had a quick off-stage costume-change between two consecutive dance routines: the first was danced barefoot and the second wearing high heels. It was a few weeks after she had won the 'Miss Tiffany' title. On stage for the second of the two routines she had felt a sharp pain in her feet sufficient to force her to drop out of the ensemble. Backstage she found blood on her feet. Someone had put needles in both her shoes. There could be no other motive than jealousy for such an act. Her flat-mates had ideas but a culprit was never proved. A few weeks later it happened again, only this time it was pieces of broken glass. The management was impassive and unhelpful. They were used to a degree of bitching in the cast, 'backbiting' as they quaintly described it in their Thai English. The third time it was super-glue in her mascara.

If Daeng had been able to find out who was responsible for these cruel tricks she might have been able to deal with the situation by confronting the culprit, or culprits. But whoever it was kept a low profile. Nagging suspicions and mental speculations were to fuel a constant anxiety that grew into depression and eventually to a state of near mental breakdown.

Disillusioned with the whole show business scene she had returned to her parents' home in Chiang Mai. Here there was a much smaller scale cabaret with a more informal, less authoritarian, system of management. The cast consisted of only sixteen dancers and while it was not completely free of backbiting there were no vicious incidents like the ones at Simon. The dancers made up a close and friendly sorority and there was evident optimism and good feeling among them. The pay was desultory. They relied critically on the 'tips' they received for posing for photographs after the show. Several of the cast worked as part-time prostitutes. In comparison with the big commercial venues this was small-time indeed. But for Daeng it was still home. She had a loving and supportive family, a comfortable room with a balcony in a spacious house with pleasant surroundings, excellent food (her mother ran weekend courses in northern Thai cooking for people from Bangkok), and old friends. Lek was by now working in Bangkok, but Malee, the other of the trio of her old school friends, was living in Chiang Mai, having settled into a stable job. Malee showed herself a constant friend at a time in Daeng's life when disillusionment was at risk of drifting into despair.

Her father was often away giving lectures in Bangkok. So the household mainly consisted of her mother, her grandmother, the silent and straw-hatted *mae barn*, or maid, two other *kathoey*, Fon and Nok, with whom Daeng shared her room, and, for some weeks, myself.

It was during these weeks, as I gained her confidence and we became friends, that Daeng was to tell me this story of her childhood and early adulthood. My introduction to her family and their invitation to me to stay at the family home are described in the introduction section of this book.

Most of Daeng's friends were *kathoey* and while I was a guest of the family, virtually all my spare time was spent in their company. For the purpose of my research this was an unexpected and exceptional opportunity, albeit one taken up at the expense of a certain amount of personal liberty. Having been accepted as a friend of the family I had the mixed privilege of no longer being spoken of and treated as a *farang*. So much so that any attempt on my part to communicate with other Westerners was, for some reason I never worked out, tacitly disapproved of and discouraged.

Duracell *Phii*

The house was spacious and the downstairs consisted of kitchen, living room, study and a large separate space, part inside, part outside, where Daeng's mother would prepare food and give her tutelage in northern Thai cooking. In addition there was a smaller room. It was full of books and family photographs, but the centrepiece was a large Buddhist shrine, bedecked with gifts and offerings of various kinds. For a while I was puzzled by this room because I never saw it used. That is, until on one occasion I found myself alone in the house with Daeng's grandmother. Conversation with her was awkward for although by this time my understanding and speaking of the Thai language was passable, she spoke a thick northern dialect that made most of what she said incomprehensible to me. But she was extremely friendly and insisted she tidy my room every day and look after my laundry. Otherwise she generally helped Daeng's mother around the house and with the preparation of the family meals. The time she was not doing these household chores she would spend watching TV or listening to a battered transistor radio which it was obvious she prized highly.

On one particular occasion I saw her fumbling and fussing with the radio and she signed to me to come and look at it. It was not working and I guessed, correctly, that it needed some new batteries. I happened to have some spare batteries which I went to fetch from my room. Returning with these I gestured to her to pass me the radio so that I could fit the new batteries. With some consternation she refused to give me the radio and it took me some while to work out that she wanted me simply to hand over the batteries and that was all. This I did and she continued to sit there impassively, holding the radio in one hand and the batteries in the other. I took this as my cue to leave, but my curiosity led me to spy on her from the open landing upstairs. She left the sitting room and went into the room with the shrine. I heard whispered incantations and guessed she was presenting the new batteries to the shrine in order that they should receive a blessing and become purged of any evil *phii*, or spirit ghosts. I waited for a short time and then came down to confront her beaming and quite happy for me to instal the batteries which I did and the radio worked fine. The shrine, with its complex images of gods, elephants, flowers, mountains and shells was a perfect monument to the successful fusion of old Animist traditions and the later Buddhist teachings. It was there for the dual purpose of appeasing potentially dangerous spirits and offering prayers and respect to the Holy One.

Vanity

I was soon to find out that the reputation *kathoey* have for *phoot mark*, talking a lot, was well founded. The members of this cast of dancers were hyperactive gossips. It seemed the only time they stopped talking was for a period when they were making up in preparation for the first show. For an hour and a half Daeng's room became a litter of costumes, make-up palettes, false eyelashes and the like and the few words spoken were solely concerned with make-up, costumes and shoes. I came to look forward to this patch of early evening peace, being able for a while to settle on the balcony outside the dressing room with a beer and write up my notes for the day.

By this time Daeng had been on medication for depression for the best part of a year. She told me she felt happier performing in the more intimate atmosphere of the smaller venue of her home town, although apparently even this had not been without its traumas. One evening, without any warning, the manager had told her she must perform one of the dance routines topless that night. This she did very reluctantly and then was nowhere to be seen until one of the others discovered her crying in the toilet. Two of the company said they didn't mind going topless in Daeng's place, and this is how the situation was resolved.

Preoccupation with clothes and appearance was constant in this troupe. Another well deserved stereotype of *kathoey* performers is that they are extremely vain. Daeng was constantly enquiring of her friends, her mother and myself whether we liked this or that dress, this or that change of hairstyle, this or that nuance of make-up and whether she should go for this or that additional cosmetic enhancement.

Collagen – 'Do I Need More?'

Seldom did a day go by without some kind of surprise or revelation in this household and this particular occasion was no exception. One night at the dinner table Daeng announced that she had made an appointment for the following day at a hospital for the enlargement of her hips. This involves the injection of collagen and she assured everyone it was a straightforward and painless procedure. The cost was 24,000 baht (£400). She asked her mother and myself if we thought it a good idea and a reasonable price to pay. I said that I thought it completely unnecessary and a waste of money. Her mother agreed with me, but we were no match for Daeng's characteristic stubbornness and the support of her *kathoey* friends Fon and Nok. Their view was that this is a low risk procedure that would increase Daeng's chances of getting work as a model or a performer. Moreover they considered it to be cheap at the price! During one last discussion her mother made a gesture which meant it would be fruitless to pursue the matter any further. Daeng had made up her mind and it was made clear that I was expected to accompany her to the clinic. I somewhat reluctantly said that as long as I was not asked to pay the bill I would do so.

After another hair-raising ride on the back of Daeng's motorcycle (she did not appear to possess the concept of sig-nalling), by some miracle we made it to what was apparent-ly a first stop at the home of a friend on the way to the hospital, pulling up at the back door of a modest house in a quiet backwater of the town. We were greeted in a pleasant fashion by two Thai women, one in her forties, the other pos-sibly her daughter. We were led into a long narrow room with a curtain track halfway down so that by pulling the curtain across it could be divided into two separate sections. The section in which we were presently standing had carpets, settees and a television and was clearly someone's living room. I was presented with a glass of fresh orange juice and politely seated on one of the settees. The two women and Daeng disappeared to the far end of the room, past the cur-tain track, and I could hear negotiations taking place in hushed tones but was unable to make out what these were about. It was only when I noticed two dubious diplomas on the wall that I realised in horror that this was indeed the 'hospital'.

The two women reappeared wearing white coats and sig-nalled for me to come down to the other end of the long room, past the curtain track in the middle. In this section was a kitchen table and chairs which appeared to have been pushed to one side, a large refrigerator and a horizontal medical examination couch complete with white sheet. My eye was drawn to a large bottle of tomato ketchup standing out amongst the other condiments on the table. This was the kitchen doubling as operating theatre.

Having been allowed to inspect the 'business end' of the long room I was led back to the living area and the curtain was pulled across so that I was unable to see into the other section where it was plain that the procedure would take place. By now thoroughly alarmed, I tried to think of a way of stopping what was about to happen, but it was too late. The silence that had descended told me that the two women were already at their work. During the half hour or so that ensued I was alone in the sitting room end scrutinising the framed certificates on the walls for some signs of authenticity. Again, without success. After this time the curtains were pulled back and the older of the two white-coated women, with a cheery smile, beckoned me to come and view the result. Wishing I was back in England I acquiesced. The only difference I could make out was a small plaster on each hip. Feeling stupid I asked Daeng if she was OK and whether she was in any pain. She indicated that everything was fine and I could see she was pleased with the result. I asked how much collagen had been used (apparently this came from France) and was told that 250ml. had been injected into each hip. 'Did I think this was enough?', I heard three voices say. By now I was speechless and nodded to indicate I thought it was enough.

The business finished, some money having changed hands, it was straight back on the motorcycle to the family home. Daeng's mother was concerned that she was feeling OK and Fon and Nok busied themselves scrutinising the result while Daeng posed, concerned to know what her friends thought and whether they considered enough collagen had been used. After long deliberations it was decided that she should have a little more injected, say some 50ml. To each hip. I protested but the others said it was fine because it had been agreed that Daeng could have more if she wished and that this would be free of charge. I again witnessed the standard post-injection procedure of Fon and Nok massaging the injected areas with crushed ice wrapped in a cloth. This was done ostensibly to spread the substance so as to simulate natural curves. The pressure exerted was as hard as she was able to stand. A few days later Fon was to be seen applying the same technique to her own face following silicone injections in four areas. Despite the denials it was evident that these procedures were not without some discomfort. But in both cases, Daeng's and Fon's, there was absolutely no talk of this at all. The only thing that concerned the recipients of these injections, obsessively, was the cosmetic result. 'Was the quantity enough?' I was repeatedly asked. My reply was always the same, 'Yes, I think it is quite enough'.

Tham Boon

Like most of the *kathoey* with whom I came into contact Daeng was a devout Buddhist. This was evident from the strict observation of daily rituals of respect. There were a range of these from a simple *wai* (an everyday gesture of supplication with the hands held, palms together, in front of a bowed head) performed to an image in passing, to a longer stop at a shrine for prayer and deliberation, to a visit to a temple whose purpose was to perform an act of merit, or *tham boon*. There was no fixed day of the week for such visits. They could be made whenever the person so wished. Daeng would go roughly once a week and on two occasions I accompanied her.

The pilgrimage to the temple had to be made in the morning. I guessed this was because, throughout the ceremony, the monk would chew and spit into a spittoon and monks are not allowed to eat after midday. The session began with the presentation of gifts together with a small denomination bank note which was discreetly presented in an envelope. Gifts were usually food or a combination of food and sundry domestic items such as cloths, containers, cleaning materials and detergents. Throughout Thailand there are shops that sell only items that are to be presented at temples, the most basic of which consists of a yellow bucket stuffed with all kinds of inexpensive dried food and everyday utilities.

The ceremony is private and has no standard liturgy or

text. The lay visitor kneels in front of the monk who utters a version of the sacred teachings whilst chewing and spitting. These may be accompanied by pronouncements about the person's present life and speculation and prediction about past and future incarnations. At the end there is a blessing and this is marked by the pouring of water from a sacred vessel over the hands and the tying of a cord around the wrist. I was able to understand only fragments of what was said. On one of the visits Daeng informed me afterwards that the monk had told her that providing she kept up her devotions she would be a complete woman in the next life, and would be able to have children. Outside the sanctuary in which this intimate ceremony took place was a woman carrying a wooden cage full of tiny birds. These can be purchased for a small sum and set free. Gifts to the monk and the setting free of a captive live creature are each acts that bestow kammic credit on the giver.

Ko Chang

Shortly after the collagen episode Daeng was asked to go to Bangkok for an interview and photocall for a monthly glossy magazine about her winning the title 'Miss Tiffany', two years earlier, and her life since this episode. She wanted to see her old school friend Lek and promised to introduce me if I accompanied her. She also wanted to call on some friends in Pattaya. I had some English and Thai friends in the coastal town of Hua Hin so it was agreed that we go together to Bangkok, see Lek, and then Daeng would go for a couple of days to Pattaya while I travelled on to Hua Hin. For me this represented a welcome break from the fascinating but sometimes very foreign-feeling world of Daeng and her circle of friends in Chiang Mai.

When Fon and Nok learned of the trip, they were not going to be left out and it was fixed that they would go with Daeng to Pattaya while I stayed with my friends in Hua Hin. We would all travel on the night train to Bangkok. This turned out an excellent choice of transport – clean, air-conditioned and inexpensive with a restaurant and bar.

Before the sleeping bunks were pulled down we watched a spectacular sunset over supper. During our conversation the three of them suggested that rather than come straight back home to Chiang Mai they show me the island of Ko Chang which is easily accessible from Bangkok and Pattaya. Ko Chang spans 490 square kilometres, much of which is Marine National Park consisting of undisturbed rain forests, abundant, often exotic wild life and clear-water beaches.

This sounded like a pleasant combination of note collecting, nature and swimming so I agreed to the plan, although I knew this would mean covering the bulk of the expenses. In the event it was well worth it. My companions were extrovert to the point of exuberance and the public's reaction to the confident way in which they carried themselves was generally warm and friendly. My introduction to Lek marked the beginning of a friendship over whose span she was to relate her story which is re-told in Chapter 7 of this book.

Since Pattaya was nearer to Ko Chang than Hua Hin I rejoined the others there. The four of us set out in the back of a cheap and very uncomfortable hired truck to the pier from which the boats departed. The woman selling tickets was a Thai in her forties and at great length went on complimenting Daeng on her beauty and asking questions about her history and family. Her son or grandson, a boy of about seven, was clearly intrigued by our party and insisted on running errands while we were waiting for our boat to arrive.

Yeepun

After the travelling we had only two days on the island and on the second of these it rained heavily and non-stop. Soon after our arrival and finding accommodation I noticed that Fon and Nok had become remote and almost conspiratorial. They would spend much of the time whispering together and go off on mysterious excursions on their own without explanation and without suggesting that Daeng or I go with them. Indeed, this was happening so often that I began to fear there was some sort of friction between the two of them and Daeng and myself. When I asked her, Daeng assured me there was not but she did not volunteer any explanation. Eventually my paranoia got the better of me and I insisted Daeng tell me what this was all about. Somewhat reluctantly, she replied with the single enigmatic word, *Yeepun*, meaning 'Japanese'.

Further fairly insistent questioning determined what was really going on. Fon and Nok, it turned out, both shared an enthusiasm for Japanese men and they were using the trip as an opportunity to conduct a little business on the side. My reaction was a mixture of amazement at the lightness with which they treated selling themselves, and relief. Thereon the whole exposé was turned into a big joke. Indeed in one restaurant I found myself acting as translator and negotiator between Fon and Nok and a group of Japanese backpackers who spoke a version of English only I seemed able to understand. I had become the 'fixer' for them both.

On the second day Daeng and myself sat inside a bar watching a wall of rain descend on the open canopy. The others were nowhere to be seen but eventually reappeared drenched and happy. Both of them had found customers.

On the return journey the same boy greeted our boat when it reached the mainland and enthusiastically helped transfer our luggage from the boat to a truck that had been commandeered. He appeared intensely interested in our group and hovered round us like a mosquito. When the truck was ready to leave he tried to clamber up to join us, to the amusement of some onlookers. Later, Daeng said she thought it likely that one day he would become a *kathoey*.

The Bakery

On our return to Chiang Mai and Daeng's house, preparations were underway for the opening of a bakery on the premises. This was another limb of Daeng's mother's culinary enterprises.

These culminated one morning in the arrival of nine monks from the local temple and an elaborate ceremony of blessings, invocations and chanting. The monks sat on cushions in a semicircle facing members of the family who knelt in front of them on the floor with hands clasped in the prayer-like gesture of respect, the *wai*, and heads respectfully bowed. Daeng sat with her family observing the rituals of the long ceremony. After about two hours the proceedings ended with a massive feast. The monks remained in their cross-legged positions and food was brought to them by everyone else present, including myself, all the time taking care to keep our heads lower than the heads of the priests.

Between the chanting and the feast a long length of string was fixed around the inside perimeter of the building. This marked out an area that was consecrated and therefore protected from the malign influences of any passing undesirable *phii*.

Daeng, Fon and Nok were devout Buddhists. The particular form of Buddhism to which they, and many others in the north, subscribed was not an intellectual one but one threaded through with superstition and the relics of ancient Animist beliefs. They all believed in *phii*, and the influence these had, or might have, in their everyday lives and those of their families. Their daily routine was punctuated with minor rituals whose purpose it was to engage the cooperation of benevolent spirits and keep at bay the harmful ones with devotions, tokens and small gifts.

I parted from the family that had made their home mine for a space of time with my own very European-style gifts. I had long since abandoned half of my research equipment – my cassette recorder – but not the other half – my daily journal. I remember thinking how absurd it would have appeared if I had produced this during my sojourn and travels with these people and asked them to talk into the microphone.

Chapter 11

Some Facts, Figures and Observations

The figures given in the box below are based on information obtained from my interviews and conversations over a period of three years with forty-three *kathoey*, aged eighteen to sixty-five (average age twenty-nine), from the towns of Bangkok, Hua Hin, Pattaya, Hat Yai, Chiang Mai and Khon Kaen.

Some Characteristics of the *Kathoey* Sample
(total number = 43)

Procedures

	Full SRS	Augmentation Mamaplasty (breast implants)	Oral Hormones
no. =	3	21	39

Age at realisation of the wish to become a woman or kathoey*

	'As long as I can remember'	≤ 7-years	≤ 11 years	≤ 15 years
no. =	6	31	40	43

Reaction within family

	Accepting	Indifferent	Hostile	(no family)
no. =	26	11	5	(1)

(* ≤: equal to or less than)

While the figures given represent an accurate record of people's reports, the following statistics relating to the total population of *kathoey* in Thailand and facts about them are not based on precise measurements. Unfortunately, samples from scientific surveys, giving precise estimates of incidence, do not exist. The latter, and the other various statistics, are estimates based on other published estimates, interviews with professors at Bangkok and Chiang Mai universities, interviews with doctors at two Sex Reassignment Surgery clinics in Bangkok, informal enquiry and my own observations. Some of these show wide variation and are given here as a spread between two extreme points. These figures and estimates apply specifically to *kathoey* as opposed to gay or homosexual men.

Incidence

Estimates of the percentage of *kathoey* in the general population of Thailand vary widely, ranging from 0.1 per cent to 0.5 per cent. A possible explanation of this variation was suggested by one of the professors at Chiang Mai University. He confirmed that large numbers of *kathoey* are to be found in the country, but this population is made up of individuals expressing different degrees of femininity. The spectrum can be thought of as ranging from the fully transgendered post-operative to the 'part time' person who dresses and performs sometimes as a man and sometimes as a woman. My own observations suggest the great majority consist in those people who have not undergone full sex reassignment surgery, either because they cannot afford it, or from simple choice, but who have nevertheless adopted the role and styles of a female full time, around which they plan and organise their lives. So perhaps a truer figure for percentage in the overall population for these individuals could be taken as the median between these two extremes, i.e. around 0.3 per cent. It is worth noting that these figures are not dissimilar to estimates of the incidence of chromosomal variants found in Klinefelter's syndrome. *Kathoey* are to be found living in every part of the country although recent patterns of migration have resulted in a greater concentration of them in the tourist towns.

Biology

There is general consensus between medical doctors that the majority of cases have a biological basis and the factors determining what makes a person a *kathoey* are in place by the age of eighteen months if not earlier. The doctors I interviewed were all of the opinion that events taking place in the womb are of primary significance. One doctor claimed there are recognisable differences in physical characteristics at birth, namely in the Adam's apple, the contour of the buttocks and characteristics of the hair. This doctor also reckoned that 65 per cent of adult *kathoey* are taller than the average Thai male.[1]

Hormones

Almost all *kathoey* take oral hormones regularly for a period of several years in their life. The composition of the dose varies.[2] Most include oestrogen and anti-androgens. The average age at which a person begins a regime of oral hormones is fifteen, but some start earlier in their school years as the drugs are readily available without prescription in chemist's shops. These hormones encourage breast development and inhibit the build up of muscle mass. They also influence the development of bone structure, hips and skin. It is unlikely that the hormones taken affect height.[3]

Sex Reassignment Surgery (SRS) Clinics

The main sex reassignment clinic in Bangkok handles between 200 and 300 cases of full SRS every year. Estimates for the number of operations carried out in Thailand are between 500 and 1,000 per year and growing.[4] Some people go to Singapore for this treatment. An estimate of the percentage of *kathoey* who opt for full SRS, based on my own sample and the figures shown here below is 6.97 per cent.

The criteria for eligibility for SRS at the main clinic in Bangkok[5] are: (a) 'to have lived as a woman for at least five years', (b) 'to have been on hormonal treatment for at least one year', and (c) 'to have been diagnosed as gender dysphoric by a psychologist'.

In the days before the legalisation of SRS, some individuals would attempt the surgery themselves with the help of a 'friend'.

Boyfriends

Most *kathoey* report having boyfriends at some point in their lives (this is not referring to short-term liaisons of prostitutes). These may be Thai, Japanese, Korean, Singaporean, Australian or Western and are predominantly individuals who identify as heterosexual.[6] Most of these men have had, or go on to have, relationships with women. While there are exceptions to the rule, *kathoey* do not have the reputation of staying in the same relationship for an extended period of time – hence the constant reference to a 'broken heart', both in their own daily gossip and in fictional accounts of them. A few establish steady relationships with foreigners mainly settling in Thailand or Singapore and very occasionally in their partner's country of origin. Having a Thai boyfriend is more common among those who become star performers – i.e. the ones who have higher status amongst them. A boyfriend's reaction to their physically ambivalent sexuality ranges from an acceptance of this to insistence on (and often financial help with) full sex reassignment surgery.

Chapter 12
Malee's Story

The life of Manat, the third of the trio of school friends, was to follow a very different course to that of Akorn and Lek. Manat was the quietest and in a sense the least ambitious of the three. He had known that he wanted to become a girl from the age of ten. When the three of them had approached Saowanee in their early teens, Daeng and Lek both expressed the desire to use whatever techniques there were available to change their physical and hormonal make-up to enhance their already feminine appearances. Manat never experienced this desire, being content to dress like a girl, assume the mannerisms of a girl, grow his hair to waist length and use spare but effective techniques of making up. Under the tutelage of Saowanee and her two helpers, he had assumed the girl's name Malee, and an appearance, while superficially more austere than the other two, was indeed striking in its way. Malee was tall and slim. She did not possess the curvaceous lines of the other two, nor did she attempt to affect the exaggerated feminine gait that the others sometimes put on. But her imposing height, waist-length hair and faintly Mona Lisa-like eyes caused heads to turn.

Staff at the school accepted Malee's transformation with the same equanimity that they showed Akorn (Daeng) and Lek. But when the time came to confront her family Malee was less fortunate. She was an only child and her father was a fiery individual. As soon as Malee appeared with Saowanee, both individuals looking obviously, though not ostentatiously, feminine, Malee's father slammed the door on the two of them and with few words dismissed the episode as a joke in very bad taste.

The following day Malee reappeared at the family home dressed in the same way. She was totally unprepared for the violence of the rage her father flew into. Her mother looked on helplessly as he let forth a tirade of anger and abuse, and used a heavy bamboo cane to beat her. Malee, badly bruised, with two broken ribs, had to spend ten days of the school holiday in hospital. But she told me that the physical pain she suffered was nothing compared to the mental anguish of her father's abrupt and seemingly terminal estrangement. She had a slight stutter which would get worse when she spoke of this terrible time in her life. Later, I was to discover from the others that this stutter first appeared after the beating from her father.

To go back to the family home after this incident was out of the question, if only for the reason that she feared a repeat of the violence. So from that time until the end of her school career she stayed with her aunt and uncle in a similarly poor village to that of her upbringing, some five kilometres from the family home.

Of the three childhood friends Malee turned out to be the most intelligent and least flamboyant. She took a degree in Business Studies and Accountancy at a specialist university in Bangkok and graduated with a top grade. Her family had no money and she was only able to do this with the help of a loan from one of the senior teachers at the school, who, since the beating from her father, had taken Malee under his wing. She was also probably the most practical of the three. Realising the difficulties *kathoey* faced when they were out of full-time education looking for jobs, she had deliberately chosen a course where the demand for qualified professionals was high. But her real love was fabrics and dress design. She could not afford the fees for night school, so in her spare time she was taught the skills of a seamstress by one of the older women of the village where she had her new home.

To the delight and relief of her mentor and benefactor at the school, and with an excellent reference from her university teacher, Malee managed to get a job in a Chiang Mai bank as soon as she graduated. It was the lowliest of positions – a junior clerk – and hardly reflected the knowledge and skills she had acquired at university. But it was an opening into a professional career that for a *kathoey* was a comparative rarity.

Notwithstanding the account of Daeng's (Akorn's) drive and determination as a schoolchild, and the leadership he had shown in the approach the three of them had made to Saowanee, by the time I met them all Malee was the one looked up to by the other two as their intellectual and emotional superior. It was the quiet and thoughtful Malee to whom they would turn in times of difficulty. Saowanee, their erstwhile 'sister', had moved to Singapore and was by this time out of their lives.

Malee's story, apart from the violent episode with her father, is less eventful and less turbulent than that of Lek and Daeng. She went directly from university to her position as clerk and did not suffer the strings of rejection and disappointment that Lek and most other *kathoey* have to face when their education comes to an end and they launch themselves into an inhospitable job market. Humble though it was for one with her qualifications, it was nevertheless a step up for a person of her social background. And, of course, in front of her stood a ladder of possible promotions if she could bring to the attention of her employers her competence and staying power at the bank.

Daeng introduced me to Malee in Chiang Mai when she was twenty-five and had been working at the bank for nearly three years. Her constancy had indeed started to pay off. She was still a clerk but held a position one notch up from her starting point. Malee completely bucked the stereotype of the loud, exhibitionist, volatile *kathoey*. She was neither vain nor spendthrift and her small but regular salary enabled her to pay all her costs of living, repay the money lent to her and have a little to spare to give to her aunt, with whom she still lived, and her mother. She did complain that she found her job a little dull at times, but she liked the security it gave and she had a lively group of friends with whom she would meet up in the evenings and weekends. Daeng of course was one of these, so I was to see a lot of Malee on these occasions. Always cool and affable, it was clear she had become the guru of the little group.

Malee's mother paid her regular visits at her sister's house where Malee was now resident. At the time I met her, Malee told me that she had only once returned to her parents' house since the *fracas* with her father. The occasion was her twenty-third birthday. There is nothing special about the age of twenty-three in Thailand. Ever since her father's outburst her mother had lived in hope of a reconciliation and had suffered continually in the absence of one. By the time Malee reached the age of twenty-three her mother felt that enough is enough and prevailed upon Malee to come to the family home and upon her husband to receive his daughter with warmth and in a spirit of reconciliation.

Malee was a regular visitor to Daeng's parents' house and it was one evening when Malee and myself found ourselves alone together in the house that the tale of this painful occasion poured out. I was suffering a mild bout of Bangkok Belly and had decided that rather than accompany Daeng and crew to the theatres that night I would stay at the house.

Malee's father had known nothing about the visit that had been planned. It was to be a surprise. This, I guessed, was partly so that her father could not pre-empt the event or take himself out. She told me how her father, stiff with embarrassment, had at first pretended to be busy. He was cold rather than hostile and had sat down with Malee for all of three minutes. The only words that were spoken between them were these, 'How old are you now, then?' Malee told him she was twenty-three. 'More like thirteen' was his reply, and that had been that.

Malee was uncharacteristically primed with emotion when she blurted out her account of this sad episode. Despite the disgraceful treatment she had received at the hands of her father, she said she still loved him, and believed that in his heart he loved her. I was also privy to a secret. Soon after she started her job at the bank, Malee had noticed that one of the bank's customers, a young Thai businessman, was taking an interest in her. Their relationship, such as it was, did not at first extend beyond friendly remarks and smiles. But several times over the last few months they had met out of office hours and he had taken her in his car to one of the *barns*, or country hotels, in the hills to the north of Chiang Mai. They were getting on well and she referred to him as her boyfriend. I was curious to know just how discreet their liaisons had to be. She said that provided they met away from the office, and for the time being outside the social milieu of the office, most people would not notice and most of those who did would turn a blind eye. Her hope was that their relationship would flourish and become a long-term one and that gradually people would come to accept them as a couple.[1]

At the time of writing Malee still works in the same job, at the same bank and still has the same Thai boyfriend. I have also heard that relations with her father have thawed, but did not like to ask if this had anything to do with her new boyfriend's bank account. She took hormone pills as they all did, but, unlike Lek and Daeng, Malee never had any desire to undergo major cosmetic surgery – breast implants or full sex reassignment surgery. She seemed fairly content with the way she looked, although slightly concerned about aspects of her face. The same evening she told me her story, she asked if I thought she needed just some 'very small' injections of silicone, indicating the regions of her cheekbone and chin. I could tell that she was planning to do this because she thought it would please her new boyfriend and I also knew that nothing I said would make a shred of difference. Nonetheless, my wary attitude prevailed and I found myself saying, yet again, 'No Malee, you have a good face and it's perfectly OK as it is'.

Postscript

In addition to their historical role as performers and entertainers, *kathoey* have found niches of employment and can be seen in ordinary jobs and places in Thai society. These are not high-profile individuals in that they do not parade in front of a public in colourful costumes like the modern cabaret performers, or set out to attract customers. Often more difficult to spot, they work in shops, markets, restaurants, studios and hotels, and a few, like Malee, in clerical professions. Khon Kaen is a large industrial town in north-east Thailand with virtually no tourists. During the week I stayed there I noticed seven *kathoey* in such jobs, including one aged sixty-five who granted me a short interview. Those whom I came across in ordinary jobs have either an androgynous appearance, or the appearance of women. They seem happy in their work and have the respect of those they work with. So despite the discrimination *kathoey* so often run up against in the open job market, some do achieve ordinary lines of work through perseverance, the help of family and friends, good fortune, or a mixture of all three.

Violent reactions from the families, usually fathers, of young *kathoey* are not uncommon but are the exception. Of the forty-three *kathoey* I spoke to, five had had problems with their families to start with, but in only one case did these remain unresolved, and this was because the father had left the family home and run off with another woman. Again, sending money back home on a regular basis was a sure fire way of causing attitudes to mellow.

Chapter 13

Kathoey *and the Religious Order*

Kathoey are often described as being religious people and as being 'involved in religious circles'.[1] Most of these make regular visits to a temple to perform an act of worship and to receive a blessing. They are received with warmth and they are clearly at home among the pagodas where they like to spend time. Enclaves of them are often located near a temple and they have traditionally been an important part of the entertainment at temple fairs. The particular brand of Buddhism they practise is an old-fashioned non-intellectual one with clear elements of Animism. Many have self-made shrines in their rooms, some modest, some elaborate. These they keep adorned with gifts and supplied with tiny bowls of rice and other foods.

On the face of it, this attendance to religious practices and closeness to holy places presents a paradox. The lives, styles, traditions and habits of a *kathoey* would seem to be the complete antithesis to those of a monk whose life, according to the Buddhist scriptures, should represent a striving for self-denial and the quenching of earthly appetites. The contrast between the two is illustrated in a list of (admittedly overlapping) descriptive labels that can be applied to each category of person, shown overleaf. Monks enjoy high status throughout the land; *kathoey*, while their grace as performers may be respected and admired, are regarded in the community at large as low-status individuals. The life of a monk is one of meditation, asceticism, learning and, in the case of senior members of the priesthood, teaching, interpreting the scriptures and offering moral guidance. That of the largely uneducated *kathoey* is one of indulgence, flamboyance and

**Contrasting Attributes and Destinies of Monk and
Kathoey***

Monk	Kathoey
Meritorious (Makers of Merit)	Non-meritorious (Recipients of de-Merit)
Meditation	Performance
Learning	Exhibitionism
Ascetic	Hedonistic
Abstemious	Indulgent
Celibate	Promiscuous
High status and respect	Low status and respect
Historically male identified	Historically female identified
Strong and admirable	Weak and pitiful
Plain dress and appearance	Exotic and glamorous
Prescriptive and proscriptive	Libertine
Ideal of dispassionate equanimity/serenity (*Chai yen*)	Passionate, turbulent and jealous (*Chai rhorn*)
Introspective	Dramatic
Redeemers	Candidates for redemption
Hindu/Buddhist origins	Animist origins

* N.B.: virtually the same attributes can be ascribed to
India's *hijra*.

performance. The insignia of the monk's calling are his
shaved head and his uniform – a simple plain robe with no
decoration; that of the *kathoey*, her exotic clothes, jewellery,
make-up and deliberately glamorous appearance. The
Buddhist scriptures express a general disdain for all forms of
sexuality and a condemnation of promiscuity. A monk is
required to remain strictly celibate. A *kathoey* is characteris-
tically a sexual libertine and, in many cases, a prostitute. A
monk must at all times remain sober and restrained in his
behaviour; the behaviour of a *kathoey* is, with justification,

caricatured as dramatic, emotionally volatile, sometimes drunk and occasionally suicidal. *Kathoey* are prone to extreme displays of emotion, running the whole gamut from hysterical anger and frustration to abject weeping. The monk is a symbol of strength and authority; the *kathoey* is a weak and pitiable creature, vulnerable as a vessel for possession by *phii*. A monk's code is prescriptive and proscriptive; a *kathoey's*, amoral.

Kathoey would seem to represent everything that the monastic system rejects and counsels against. But they have never been censored, let alone persecuted, by the priesthood. Both monks and *kathoey*, it seems, enjoy a recognised and legitimate place in the wider community. Furthermore, the two appear to have coexisted for centuries, not only harmoniously, but with a degree of mutual respect and co-operation. How can this be? It is in this paradox that the key to the true historical place of *kathoey* in the Thai community is perhaps to be found.

The contrast between the two sets of characteristics is indeed striking. It seems so complete that it would be possible theoretically to derive the life, habits and characteristics of a *kathoey*, given those of a monk, by applying a simple rule of inversion. Conversely, it would seem possible to derive the life of a monk from that of a *kathoey* in the same manner. The one is an opposite imprint of the other.

Why do monks therefore not dissociate themselves from *kathoey* and regard them as sinners? The answer is to be found in the Buddhist account of what causes a person to be born a *kathoey*.

Buddhists believe in reincarnation. The individual can be reborn an indefinite number of times, and must strive in his or her present life to make merit through self-denial, suffering and the priesthood. Eventually, if sufficient merit is accumulated, he/she is no longer reborn having attained the ideal state of *nibbana*[2] – spiritual peace, or one-ness. In what form the individual is reborn depends upon his performance – i.e. his success in gaining merit –in a previous life. *Kathoey* are born as they are because they were promiscuous, and therefore makers of demerit, in a previous life. Under the Buddhist creed being born a *kathoey* is the person's sentence for their previous transgressions. Furthermore, if one is born a *kathoey* one is lumbered with all the baggage of attributes that goes with the role. Even their beauty and therefore their attractiveness to men can under this light be regarded as something of a curse.

Born *kathoey*, individuals cannot escape their attributes. They are bound for a life of unhappiness and promiscuity, for which, theoretically, they are not in this life open to criticism or moral censorship, simply because it is their destiny. When a spirit medium is temporarily possessed by a *phii* for the duration of a trance she becomes *maa khii* – a 'horse to ride'. The actions she commits and the statements she makes throughout this period of time are not attributed to her, but to the spirit that is in possession of her. So she can get as drunk, as abusive and as rude as she wants without any discredit or criticism backfiring on her. The plight of *kathoey* is somewhat similar, except theirs is a condition that lasts for life (at least for this life) rather than for a short time. She is subject to desires and drives which are regarded not as the direct result of possession by a *phii* but as a direct result of misdeeds in a previous life. And these she is too weak to resist. Therefore, while sexual excess is disapproved of by the priesthood and promiscuity is theoretically taboo in the community at large, these, as well as the other excesses, are tolerated in the *kathoey* population because this group of people *cannot help being what they are*. It is in this sense that *kathoey* are traditionally accepted as a part of the community.

Precisely because the two are total opposites does the relationship between monk and *kathoey* run deep. It is a symbolic and symbiotic one. Put crudely, it suits *kathoey* to be an acknowledged and accepted part of the community, albeit it technically a low status one. But it also suits the monastic system for there to be a group of individuals, on display as it were, sometimes literally, that exemplifies the converse of everything the Buddhist scriptures teach. Here are a group of unfortunates suffering the terrible punishment of being born as women in bodies that are more like men's.

Kathoey therefore provide the priesthood with a living, walking, negative model against which the priestly virtues can fluoresce. In return, the monks provide *kathoey* with the sanctuary of a recognised role within the community which is reinforced by a certain amount of day-to-day interaction and co-operation.[3]

Chapter 14

Changing Attitudes – East and West

The West

Shock-horror was the reaction of Catholic explorers of the Middle Ages when they encountered an unclassifiable gender in native North American tribes and in the Philippines. To them this was plainly the work of the devil: there could be no other possible explanation. The reaction of the British raj in India when they came across colonies of *hijra* was much the same. The missionaries of the mid nineteenth century from America and England took a softer view of transgendered folk. American Presbyterian Dr McGilvary and his wife viewed the *kathoey* they encountered in northern Siam as 'freaks of nature' – people to be pitied rather than condemned and legislated against. To anthropologists of the late nineteenth and early twentieth centuries the presence of *berdache* among native American Indian tribes was a phenomenon to be observed and documented, not judged. But to them it was something of tangential rather than central interest. The major writers of the day were much more interested in constructing grandiose theories of family and kinship.

Transgender was also largely ignored in the theories of Darwin and Freud, not surprisingly, perhaps, in Darwin's case, as his ideas were concerned with reproduction and the evolution of species. Freud's theories of unconscious motives and repressed desires, it is now widely held, are somewhat 'Eurocentric' and should be read and applied very much in context of their time and place in history. Even the radical modernist writers of mid twentieth-century France did not address the issue of transgender from anything other than a European perspective. Only very recently – in the past twenty or thirty years – probably as a result of feminist and post-feminist writers, has gender and its related issues been direct-ly addressed by scholars as a subject of importance in its own right. The appearance of 'Gender Studies' as a subject in uni-versity curricula, and the launch of new international jour-nals[1] specifically devoted to the study of gender issues, mark the arrival of a fresh debate with a global perspective and an interdisciplinary forum. The *Intersex Society of North America* is a recently formed organisation that vociferously opposes the medical assignment of gender at birth in the case of babies born with ambiguous sex organs.

Such has been the abiding strength through the centuries of a binary model of male and female: a model essential to cultures and moralities build on Judaeo-Christian axioms. How completely different to the primitive Animist belief that gender is not rigid but plastic; while male and female are surely the main players, there can nevertheless be different colours and shades and these are naturally to be integrated rather than expelled. And how different was the attitude of the bearers of Hindu and Buddhist philosophies when they began to attract a following. These religions appear to have had no difficulty in accommodating the Animist ideas of a third gender and indeed up to a point adapting their mythologies, images and practices in the cause of compatibility.

But, if we look very closely at the fabric of our Western societies, some interesting anomalies are to be seen, some-times in the unlikeliest of places. Odd examples in literature and in everyday life appear that are quite out of line with the orthodoxy of the time. Laslo Kürti, writing about tradition-al East European societies, remarks,

> . . . however patriarchal East European societies have been, men and women created special occasions to under-mine implicit assumptions about gender systems and to contest the roles and rules assigned to them by the state, the Church, and masculinised institutions. I am specifical-ly interested in how these practices – although few and far between – allow individuals to release pent-up frustrations

by enabling them to act out their desires, or misgivings, in a socially sanctioned arena.[2]

Winifred Schleiner, professor of English at the University of California, points out that the romantic literature of the Renaissance contains quite a few examples in which a male puts on female clothes 'for reasons of intrigue, love stratagem, or escape from danger', and, what is more, succeeds in impressing other characters with his beauty.[3]

In medieval England and France, the dress and general appearance of page boys could be construed as not entirely consistent with the ideal of manhood which prevailed at the time. And Shakespeare's girls were, of course, always played by boys. Shakespeare uses gender confusion many times as a dramatic device. In *Twelfth Night*, for example, Viola, the romantic heroine of the play, as part of the plot has to pretend she is a boy. Here is a doubly confused situation in that a boy actor plays a girl whose role in the play is to masquerade as a boy.

Such examples are isolated, or 'few and far between' as Kürti puts it, in that they exist in pockets dissociated from the mainstream flow of life, for example in carnivals or in literature or in theatre. They do not pose a threat to the prevailing orthodoxy because they operate under a special licence, as it were. In Europe and America the ideal of the seasoned, heroic, controlling male continued on into the nineteenth and twentieth centuries, arguably reaching new heights in the all-male English boarding school of the 1930s, 1940s and 1950s. Here the cult of muscular Christianity ruled supreme with its regime of cold showers, fagging, beatings and countless other harsh devices. The justification for these unpleasant and often cruel traditions was that they were 'character building'. By being taken away from the warmth and support of the family home and put through an assault course of privation and humiliation the individual would achieve a level of manhood and leadership that was considered so desirable at the time.

Much of the curriculum in these places was devoted to a classical education, concentrating on Latin, Greek and

History at the expense of Science, Technology and Art. Teaching methods emphasised more the rote memory of names and dates than an understanding of the social contexts in which historical lives and events were played out. The stultifying range of subjects taught, the anti-intellectual methods of teaching and the barrack-like living conditions were designed to make a man of you: at best a stiff-upper-lipped, stoical kind of a man but at worse, and alas, more frequently, an insensitive and short-sighted one.[4]

Yet within these extreme regimes were to be found pockets of activity that would appear totally to go against the authoritarian ethic. For example, it was perfectly permissible, expected even, for younger boys to take girls' parts in school plays. In many of these schools it was not uncommon for an older boy to form a protective friendship with a younger (often feminine-looking) boy. The oases of humanity that these innocent instances of patronage represented were regularly part of the social fabric of these institutions even though they were completely at odds with the main flow.[5]

What are we to make of this picture of a sweepingly enforced tradition of male-female dimorphism down through the ages of Christian Europe, with isolated, unexplained, but tacitly approved, breaks in the tradition? Perhaps an inclination in a minority of people to cross male-female gender boundaries is not after all something peculiar to those exotic cultures in which it is regarded as a normal part of everyday life. The very severity of the reactions of the pious upholders of Christian beliefs when they encountered a third sex in foreign parts might be interpreted (speculatively) as a defensive reaction on their part; a Freudian denial of a gender-ambiguous element in their own culture – even, conceivably, in their own psyche. Repressed feelings and thoughts are known to find expression in oblique and symbolic ways. So perhaps the unusual behaviour at carnivals like those to which Kürti and others have alluded, the references to androgeny and cross-dressing in Renaissance literature, boys acting girls on the stage and the hidden quasi-romantic rituals of the public school function as escape valves in an environment hostile to any deviation from a strict black and white vision of two robust genders.

Transgender was not an issue that could even be opened in the history of the West because traditional Christian ideology teaches that God created Man and Woman for the sacred purpose of procreation, within marriage, in His own image. By definition, procreation had to remain at the very core of the ideology.

Not until the hippy days of the 1960s did the West see the beginnings of any real cultural departure from traditional male/female stereotypes and the idea that the sacred purpose of sex was procreation, not enjoyment. And only with the arrival, subsequently, of ideas from the feminist movement did the age-old tradition of gender-appropriate behaviour defined in terms of the biological sex a person was assigned at birth, come in for some serious debate.

The late twentieth century witnessed the first major challenge to the old gender stereotypes. Camp comedy was heard for the first time on the radio in ground-breaking programmes such as the BBC's *Round The Horne* in the 1950s. Soon this was to become a popular style of entertainment in the theatre and on the television screen.

And it was only in the 1980s that a grass-roots movement of people identifying themselves as transgender emerged in America and Europe. The first clinics opened offering cosmetic techniques of altering a person's outward appearance so as to bring this in line with their psychological identification. It is interesting that these developments lagged behind the discovery of Klinefelter's Syndrome in America in 1942. Any publicity given to a genetically ambiguous form of human being would not have sat comfortably with the wartime regimes of this period and the paranoid McCarthy years of the 1950s.

Why is transgender and the cult of 'ladyboys' widely regarded as something more common in Thailand than in any other country? The preceding observations may provide a clue. The naturally smooth skin and feminine figures and features of some Thai boys make it a relatively simple matter for them to change their outward appearance so as to look like girls. And the growth of the tourist industry may well provide an incentive for some of these people to earn a living by entering the ranks of the so-called 'ladyboy' performers. But we have seen that *kathoey* have a much longer history than that of the 'ladyboys' of the commercial cabarets. What, more than anything else, facilitates the movement across gender boundaries is the atmosphere of tolerance and the absence of censorship which the ambient social and religious environment provides. On this theory we might expect to find examples of transgender in other cultures where political censorship, overt or covert, is not applied. Sure enough, this would generally seem to be the case. So this question can be turned around to ask, 'what are the conditions under which the crossing of gender boundaries is taboo?' And the answer lies in the proscription that is deeply rooted, historically, morally and, most of all, religiously, in those cultures in which it is not apparent. But look at some of the rituals of these cultures with a microscope and then it *is* visible, albeit in double disguise, in the carnivals referred to by Kürti, in boys playing girls on the stage, in short, in a spectrum of social microcosms in which it may be camouflaged and contained.

The continuance of transgender in other cultures whose Animist roots are undisturbed by the prevailing religious doctrine, and the symbolic and sometimes hidden manifestations in cultures where it is disallowed, suggest that a transgender or 'third-sex' class may be no more endemic to Thailand than to anywhere else. It is just more openly exhibited there. The relatively recent emergence of cosmetic clinics and public forums for discussion of transgender in the West may herald its eventual liberation. The fact that this new openness is contiguous with a faltering adherence to the Christian faith adds weight to the theory that the Christian doctrine has performed as a powerful inhibitor of anything other than a strictly binary version of sex/gender. Has it really taken us two millennia to get back to an ancient Animist perspective on these issues?

Modern Thailand

Paradoxically, as attitudes in the Western world veer towards a greater understanding and tolerance of people who experience gender dysphoria, attitudes of the Thai authorities appear to be swinging in the opposite direction.

The roots of global business in modern Thailand now run deep. Bangkok has become a modern cosmopolitan city. The tourist industry is vital to the Thai economy. To preserve and expand it, the authorities are increasingly keen to promote an image of the country that is calculated to appeal to foreigners as contemporary and wholesome. The highly successful promotion of 'Amazing Thailand'[6] is of a land of smiles where the people are friendly, the sights are dazzling, the beaches are clean, the food is delicious and the streets are safe. All true enough, maybe, but the image is palpably incomplete, as anyone familiar with the night life of Bangkok and other tourist towns will know. There are sporadic initiatives to clean up the country's image. For example a 2 a.m. curfew has been imposed on most bars and clubs. But the sex industry (although still technically illegal) is, of course, far too valuable to the country's economy for there to be any firm-handed discouragement.

The presence on the streets, in the shops, in the restaurants and in the bars, of people who appear to be neither men nor women would seem to have no place in the revised, Westernised, version of the country that the authorities are so keen to project. The new regime inclines to the surreptitious removal of undesirables, which category has come to include *kathoey*, from the public eye, wherever possible. It is indeed a baleful sight to watch these people being herded by police on to the back of a truck late at night on the Sukumvit Road, bound for an overnight stay in the 'monkey house'. *Kathoey* would seem to have no place in 'Amazing Thailand'. The current authorities would like to pretend they do not exist and this means keeping them as far as possible out of sight of foreign visitors.

Thailand's *kathoey* are as much a part of that country's cultural heritage as any other tradition. People of the hill tribes in the north proudly parade themselves in front of the tourists in their ethnic costume. Coach loads of visitors descend upon the silk weavers to see them show off their craft. A visit to one of Bangkok's famous floating markets is on all the tourist agenda. But the position of *kathoey* as an indigenous and long-standing part of the cultural furniture, as contextual to the Buddhist doctrine, as traditionally accepted, admired, pitied and even sometimes held in awe, is swept aside in the current attempt to recast the country in a mould calculated to be blandly appealing to Westerners. In the commercial theatres such as Alcazar and Tiffany they are allowable as a kind of curiosity for visitors to gawk at – almost a freak show. But on the streets and in other public places they have become an embarrassment. Consequently the petty thieving that is practised by no more than a very small minority, and is no more common than in the population at large, is seized upon and exaggerated in media propaganda as another device to single out *kathoey* and cast them in an unfavourable light. Not surprisingly, there is considerable resentment among them over this unfair treatment.

The concept of 'gay' did not appear in Thailand until the 1960s and did not enter into common parlance until the 1970s and 1980s, and then almost exclusively in Bangkok among the moneyed middle classes. It was entirely a Western import and was not at first easily assimilated into a wider Thai language and culture. A sexual relationship between two men both of whom identify as men has no acknowledged place in traditional Thai village life. So a Westerner's claim to be a 'gay man' was met with some bewilderment because the two words represented a *non-sequitur* in the Thai order.[7] It was also regarded with fear and suspicion because of the widely published association of gayness with HIV and AIDS during the 1970s and 1980s. *Kathoey* represented an old and familiar tradition and their orientation and activities were understood on the grounds that they were not men, they were *kathoey*.

But as the country comes increasingly under the influence of international commerce and its major towns become infinitely more cosmopolitan in character, so the credibility of the newcomer category of gays has gained ground and even a certain respectability. And among the middle classes of Bangkok who have latched on to the concept of gayness as modern, Western and trendy, the old concept of *kathoey* begins to appear quaint and uncool. Many middle-class Thai gays now consider themselves to be socially superior to *kathoey* and the two groups do not easily mix. Ironically, now, in the major cities, a subculture little more than thirty years old (gay) is strongly in the ascendant while an ancient one (*kathoey*), whose history spans hundreds, possibly thousands, of years is being marginalised and threatened with displacement.

The double irony is that while transgender increasingly becomes an issue of interest and discussion in the West, and (if the advertisements in London telephone kiosks are anything to go by) an increasingly popular source of sexual recreation, it is being dismissed by the Thai authorities and the new generation of white-collar workers as out of sync with the modern age as they see it. This perception of what is 'modern' in the Western world would therefore seem to be naïvely running about thirty years out of date. That *kathoey* should presently be facing a persecution not dissimilar to that inflicted on transgender groups by the old colonial powers, *but by their own people*, is indeed a sad state of affairs.

Chapter 15
Old Age

Over a year has passed since I first met Lek and we had sat on a bench in Dusit Park where she told me the story of Big Mitch and the Green Papaya Bar in Patpong. Now we sit on deck chairs, side by side, beneath a canopy of parasols, sunlight spilling through the gaps where they don't quite meet. We are on the beach of the crazy tourist town of Pattaya. We watch and make unkind comments as a somnolent traffic of overweight *farang* and their young Thai escorts flows along the water's edge. Lek unconsciously cups her left hand over each of her new breasts. She had gone to Singapore for the job and it had cost $US 600. It was the last of the money she had received from Mitch. They were no longer in touch.

She has no regrets. Her six-month-old breasts now feel as much a part of her as her arms and legs. They *are* her. She tries to recall her previous body and the small products of over a decade of taking oral hormones. The doctor had said she was ready for implants and she should rest from the hormones for a while and take vitamins instead.

I ponder the infinity of the sea and sand and know that my researches, such as they are, will never be complete, but that they must draw to some kind of a close. I shall never quite know what goes on behind those black eyes and in the minds of Lek's numerous counterparts. She has her small tin of rice at the ready in order to appease the spirits of the mosquitoes when it starts to get dark.

There is another question I need to ask. I had seen very few elderly *kathoey* on my travels: two in Chiang Mai and one in Khon Kaen. The long haired sixty-five-year-old shop-worker in Khon Kaen, who wore an Alice band, agreed to talk to me through an interpreter, but would not agree to be photographed. From talking to her, and some others in Chiang

Mai, and from Walter Irvine's account of spirit mediums, I knew they were there in the community, but they were not as accessible to the researcher as the younger generation.

I turn to Lek who is gazing at the line where sea meets sky. One final question for this researcher. In English.

'Lek.'

'Mmm.'

'What happens to *kathoey* when they get old? When they are not beautiful any more?'

Her round face stares back at me in astonishment. How can *farang* be so stupid?

'They sleep, Richar', saleep. Co' they no ha' money.'

A not totally unexpected question for me too. From Lek: 'Beautiful Richar', or not?'

Subsequent research was to prove that Lek's somewhat terse description of what happens to *kathoey* when they become old does not give anything like the full picture. The careers of those who enter a life of prostitution the age of twenty or younger are reckoned to be pretty well over by the age of thirty, as is the case for women prostitutes. Then, maybe, if they have no families to return to, or if their families will not have them, and if they have not saved enough money to live on (which is more than likely), they may well lapse into a state of passivity, doing little apart from lounging around, watching the TV and gossiping – 'sleep' as Lek describes it. In Western countries such a state might be labelled 'depression' and considered undesirable. But in south-east Asia prolonged inactivity and drifting are not necessarily regarded as abnormal, dishonourable or pathological. Many of those who find themselves in low demand because they are no longer able to compete with their younger counterparts naturally form themselves into what we might call 'support groups', sharing a room, picking up occasional work – living a frugal, communal life.

What percentage of *kathoey* enter prostitution, either by choice or through economic necessity, is not clear. Some, like Daeng, become performers, even stars. And among these a certain number engage in casual sex work as a sideline. In this respect they are not unlike the lower-ranking show-girls of nineteenth-century Europe who were famed for their moral looseness. In the case of professional performers, when they become too old to take on the more glamorous roles, there are a number of work options. They may be given comic or buffoonish parts to play in the cabaret. They may be employed off stage as seamstresses, set designers or assistant choreographers. Or they may help with the administration of the venue.

But while they enjoy a reputation, indeed a cultural tradition, as providers of amorous services, not all *kathoey* lead lives of full-time or part-time promiscuity. Some, like Malee in this account, find themselves holding down ordinary jobs and living with a 'sister' or a husband. Rarely are they to be found living alone.

Such is the fate of these damaged unresolved yet courageous souls.

Notes and References

Introduction

1. Harré, R. and Secord, P.F., *The Explanation of Social Behaviour*, Oxford: Blackwell, 1972.

2. *Farang*, with the 'r' pronounced halfway between the English 'r' and 'l', is a common semi-slang Thai term for Westerners and is derived from *farangset* meaning 'French'.

Chapter 1: Rama V School

1. The statistic actually given to me by a senior teacher at the school was 'between 5 and 10 per cent'. This was also confirmed by a pupil of a similar size secondary school in Khon Kaen. It is worth noting that these schools are in the north and north-east of the country, where the old traditions might be expected to last longest.

2. A good account of the traditions and career of a Geisha is to found in Arthur Golden's novel, *Memoirs of a Geisha*, London: Chatto & Windus, 1997.

Chapter 2: Chiang Mai University

1. This is a very common feature of both traditional and modern Thai dance and can be seen today throughout the country.

Chapter 3: Biological Accidents

1. U. Mittwoch, in *Genetics of Sex Differentiation*, New York: Academic Press, 1973, writes, 'It is a striking fact that all vertebrate embryos, whatever their sex chromosome constitution, originally develop the basis of both male and female sex organs. The process of sex differentiation originates in the hermaphroditic condition and consists of the progressive development of the organs of one sex at the expense of the other . . . Immediately after being formed, the gonads pass through an apparently undifferentiated state and

contain the forerunners of both ovarian and testicular tissue.'

2. See, for example, Caroline Hawkridge, *The Menopause, HRT and You*, London: Penguin Books, 1999.

3. Money, J. and Ehrhardt, A.A., *Man & Woman, Boy and Girl: The Differentiation and Dimorphism of Gender Identity from Conception to Maturity.* Baltimore: Johns Hopkins University Press, 1972.

4. The ethics behind this standard 'treatment' of babies born with non-uniform sex organs has recently come in for some vociferous criticism, in particular from the Intersex Society of North America (*www.isna.org*).

5. Hill, W.W., 'Note on the Pima Berdache'. *American Anthropologist,* 66, no. 6, pt. 1, 1964 (pp. 1288–99).

6. See Ramet, S. (ed.), *Gender Reversals & Gender Cultures: Anthropological and Historical Perspectives.* London and New York: Routledge, 1996.

7. Lang, S., 'There is More Than Just Women and Men. Gender Variance in North American Indian Cultures.' In Ramet, S. (ed.), *op. cit.*

8. Ramet, S. (ed.), *op. cit.*, p. 185.

9. Money, J. and Ehrhardt, AA. *op. cit.*

10. Andersson, S., Berman, D.M., Jenkins, E.P. and Russell, D.W., 'Deletion of steroid 5 alpha-reductase 2 gene in male pseudo-hermaphroditism', *Nature*, 354, 159–61, 1991.

11. Soerensen, K., *Klinefelter's Syndrome in Childhood, Adolescence and Youth: A genetic, clinical, developmental, psychiatric & psychological study*, Parthenon, 1987. An informative and well supported information sheet about Klinefelter's Syndrome is also available on the Internet: 'What is Klinefelter's Syndrome?', by Steve, R. Hammett for the Klinefelter's Organisation U.K. 1998. *http://members.aol.com/klinefelterorg/whatis.htm.*

12. Mittwoch, U., *op. cit.*

13. Hawkridge, C., *op. cit.*

14. Bolin, A., 'Traversing Gender', in Ramet, S. (ed.), *op. cit.*

15. Zhou, J.-N, Hofman, M.A., Gooren, L.J. and Swaab, D.F., 'A Sex Difference in the Human Brain and its Relation to Transexuality', *Nature*, 387, 68–70, 1995.

16. Green, R., *(unpublished paper)*

17. Alvar Nuñez Cabeza de Vaca. *La relación y comentarios del gouernador Aluar Nuñez Cabeza de Vaca, de lo acaescido en las dos jomadas que hizo a las Indias, Valladolid, 1555.*

18. Hammett, S.R., 'What Is Klinefelter's Syndrome?', *op. cit.*

19. Mortimer, R., *Gender Trouble* (working title). 25-minute film telling the medical and personal histories of four intersex people. Wonderdog Productions. In preparation.

20. Marre, J. (producer and director), *Lady Boys*. London: Harcourt Films, Production in association with TVF and BBC Channel 4, 1992.

21. Divorce is generally a taboo subject in Thailand. Often when a person says their father is 'dead' this means he has deserted the family for another woman.

Chapter 4: Saowanee's Plan

1. These ages at which a conscious wish was expressed by the three friends to become a girl are not untypical among *kathoey* (see Chapter 11).

Chapter 5: Buddhism and a Third Sex

1. Mills, M.B., 'Attack of the Widow Ghosts: Gender, Death and Modernity in Northeast Thailand', in Aihwa Ong and Michael G. Peletz (eds.), *Bewitching Women, Pious Men: Gender and Body Politics in Southeast Asia*. Berkeley: University of California Press. 1995.

2. Schouten, J., *A Description of the Government, Might, Religion, Customes, Traffick and other Remarkable Affairs of Siam*. Historical Archives Services, Bangkok: Chalermnit Press, 1969 (facsimile of 1636 original).

3. *Karma and nirvana are* the Sanskrit forms, *kamma* and *nibbana*, their Pali (more colloquial) equivalents. The latter forms are the ones used in this book.

4. Davids, R.T.W. and Stede, W. (eds.)., *Pali-English Dictionary*. New Delhi: Oriental Books Reprint Corporation, 1975.

5. Khamhuno (pseud.), *Gay Prakot Nai Wongkan Song (Gays Appear in Sangha Circles)*. Sankhom Satsana (Religion and Society Column). *Siam Rath Sutsapta* (Siam Rath Weekly). vol. 36, no. 22, 18 Nov. 1989.

6. Bunmi Methangkun, *Khon Pen Kathoey Dai Yang-rai? (How Can People Be Kathoey?)*. Bangkok: Abhidhamma Foundation, 1986. (n.b. It is a Thai tradition to refer to authors by their first names rather than their surnames).

7. *Vinaya*, vol 1, p. 768.

8. Bunmi, *op. cit.*

9. Suchip Punyanuphap. *Phra Traipidok Samrap Prachachon (The Tipitaka for the People)*, Bangkok: Mahamakut Ratchawittayalai, 1982.

10. Manit Manitcharoen, *Photjananukrom Thai (Thai Dictionary)*, Bangkok: Ruam-san, 1983.

11. Jackson, P.A., *Dear Uncle Go. Male Homosexuality in Thailand* Bangkok: Bua Luang Books, 1995, p. 194.

12. Jackson, *op. cit.*, p. 193.

13. Bunmi, *op. cit.*

14. Jackson, *op. cit.*, p. 258.

15. Prasok (pseud.)., 'Khang Wat' ('Beside the Monastery Column'), *Siam Rath*, Bangkok, 2 March, 2532, 1989, p. 10.

16. Bunmi, *op. cit.*

17. Jackson, *op. cit.*

Chapter 6: The Kathoey of Modern Thailand and Old Siam

1. Wood, W.A.R., *A history of Siam from the earliest times to the year A.D. 1781 with a supplement dealing with more recent events*. Bangkok: 1959 Chalermnit Press. (facsimile of original, 1926).

2. Wood, W.A.R., *Land of Smiles*, Bangkok: Krundebarnagar Press, 1935.

3. Wood, W.A.R., *Consul in Paradise. Sixty-nine years in Siam*. London: Souvenir Press, 1965 (orig. Trasvin Publications).

4. Herdt, G. (ed.), *Third Sex, Third Gender. Beyond Sexual Dimorphism in Culture and History*. New York: Zone Books 1994 (Introductory chapter).

5. Nanda, S., *Neither Man nor Woman. The Hijras of India*. Wadsworth: International Thomson Publishing, 1999.

6. *Ibid.*

7. Personal communication with professors at Thammasat University, Bangkok and Chiang Mai University.

8. Jackson, P.A., *op. cit.* (Chapter 5), pp. 192–3.

9. For an anthropologist's account of the rise of the entertainment industry in south-east Asia see Manderson, L. and Jolly, M. (eds.), *Sites of Desire, economies of pleasure: sexualities in Asia and the Pacific*, Chicago and London: University of Chicago Press, 1977.

10. Schouten, J., *op. cit.*, (Chapter 5).

11. Bowring, J., *The Kingdom & People of Siam*, Oxford:

Oxford University Press, 1969 (facsimile of nineteenth-century original).

12. Smyth, H.W., *Five Years in Siam – from 1891–1896*, Bangkok: White Lotus, 1994 (facsimile of original, 1898).

13. American Presbyterians Dr Daniel McGilvary (1858–1911) and his wife Sophia were foremost among the pioneer missionaries, educators and innovators of this time. McGilvary, D. *A half-century among the Siamese and the Lao: an autobiography.* New York and London: Fleming H. Revell, 1912.

14. Seidenfaden, E. makes precisely the same observation, 'In former days, a generation or more ago, both sexes dressed in the *phanung* or loin cloth (the *languti* of Indian origin), and this with the fashion of both men and women cutting their hair short might have made it difficult for new comers to distinguish males from females.' (In 'The Origins and Habitats of the Thai Peoples', *The Siam Society*, Bangkok, 1958.)

Chetana Nagavajara has referred to a 'disregard for male robustness, and a bent for "effeminacy" on the construction of the hero figure' in Thai classical literature *'Unsex Me Here': An Oriental's Plea for Gender Reconciliation. Warasan Mahawwitthayalai Silapakorn* 12 (special issue).

15. Wood, W.A.R., *Land of Smiles, op. cit.*

16. Hallett, H.S., *A Thousand Miles on an Elephant in the Shan States*, Edinburgh and London: William Blackwood & Sons, 1890.

17. Hallett, H.S., *op. cit.*, p. 99.

18. Smyth, H.W., *op. cit.*

19. Irvine, W., *The Thai-Yuan 'Madman' and the 'modernizing, developing Thai nation' as bounded entities under threat: a study in the replication of a single image.* Ph.D. thesis, School of Oriental and African Studies, London, 1982.

20. Buls, C., *Croquis Siamois*, Brussels: Georges Balat, 1901. (English language version, *Siamese Sketches*, translated by Walter E.J. Tips, Bangkok: White Lotus, 1994).

21. Buls, C., *op. cit.* (trans.), p. 40.

22. Orgibet, J., *From Siam to Thailand. Backdrop to the Land of Smiles*, Kofco (Thailand) Ltd, 1982.

23. Marre, J., *op. cit.* (Chapter 3).

24. Balzer, M.M., 'Sacred Genders in Siberia. Shamans, bear festivals and androgeny', in Ramet, S.P. (ed.), *op. cit.* (Chapter 3).

Andaya, L.Y., 'The Bissu. Study of a Third Gender in Indonesia.' Unpublished paper presented to the 1998 conference at Honolulu, University of Hawaii, *Engendering the History of Early Modern Southeast Asia.*

Brewer, C., 'Baylan, Asog. Transvestism, and Sodomy: Gender, Sexuality and the Sacred in Early Colonial Philippines'. *Intersections: Gender, History and Culture in the Asian Context,* *http://wwwsshe.murdoch.edu.au/intersections,* 2 August 2001.

Lang, S., 'There is More than Just Women and Men', in Ramet S. (ed.), *op. cit.* (Chapter 3).

25. Totman, R.G., *Social Causes of Illness,* London: Souvenir Press, 1979.

26. Curtis, L.J., *The Laos of North Siam,* Philadelphia: The Westminster Press, 1903.

27. Irvine, W., *op. cit.*

28. Balzer, M.M., *op. cit.*

29. Klausner, W.J., *Reflections of Thai Culture,* Bangkok: The Siam Society, 1993.

30. Allyn, E., *Trees in the Same Forest: Thailand's Culture and Gay Subculture (The Men of Thailand Revisited),* San Francisco: Bua Luang Books, 1991.

31. Marre, J., *op. cit.*

32. Jackson, P.A., *op. cit.* (Chapter 5), p. 195.

33. Jackson, P.A., *op. cit.* (Chapter 5), p. 199.

34. *Satree Lex (The Iron Ladies).* Yongyoot Thongkongtoon (Director). Thai Entertainment, March 2000.

Chapter 7: Lek's Story

1. *Satree Lex, op. cit.* (Chapter 6).

2. A notorious example is that of Mark Cookson an ex-London cab driver and divorcee who confesses he was unaware that the girl whom he had met in the late 1980s in Bangkok, Christie, was a *kathoey* who had undergone full SRS. When she told him the truth he at first reacted with anger and dismay, walking away from the situation. But after a few day's reflection he returned to her. Since this time they have been living together in Ko Samui running a successful business in the form of a bar and cabaret called *Christies.*

3. In places such as the grounds of temples and hotels different types and sizes of palm trees are sometimes deliberately planted and cultivated so that their positions and juxtapositions have a particular symbolic, or mystical significance. The result can be eerily effective, especially in the light tropical breeze of the early evening when the swaying and dipping movements of the large leaves can appear both human and supernatural.

Chapter 8: The Sex Industry in Thailand

1. Report of the International Labour Organisation (ILO), 1998.

2. Orgibet, J., *op. cit.* (Chapter 6).

3. Shearer, A., *Thailand, The Lotus Kingdom.* London: John Murray, 1989.

4. Cummings, J., *Thailand*, London, Melbourne, Oakland: Lonely Planet Publications, 1999.

5. Shearer, A. *op. cit.*

6. Cummings, J. *op. cit.*

7. Brown, L. *Sex Slaves. The Trafficking of Women in Asia*, London: Virago 2000. pp. 83–85.

8. Saengtienchai, C., Knodel, J., Vaniandingham, M. and Pramualratana, A., '"Prostitutes Are Better Than Lovers": Wives Views on the Extramarital Sexual Behaviour of Thai Men'. In Jackson, P.A. and Cook, N.M. (eds.) *Genders and Sexualities in Modern Thailand.* Silkworm, Chiang Mai, 1999.

9. Jackson, P.A., *op. cit.* (Chapter 5).

Chapter 9: Transgender in Other Cultures

1. Hekma, G., 'A female soul in a male body', in Herdt, G. (ed.), *op. cit.* (Chapter 6).

2. Nanda, S., *op. cit.* (Chapter 6).

3. Andaya, L.Y., *op. cit.* (Chapter 6).

4. Besnier, N., 'Polynesian Gender Liminality', in Herdt, G. (ed.), *op. cit.* (Chapter 6).

5. Brewer, C., *op. cit.* (Chapter 6).

6. Balzer, M.M., *op. cit.* (Chapter 6).

7. Alvar Nuñez Cabeza de Vaca, *op. cit.* (Chapter 3).

8. Gunson, N., *Messengers of Grace: Evangelical Missionaries in the South Seas 1797–1860.* Melbourne: Oxford University Press, 1978.

9. Besnier, N., *op. cit.* (Chapter 6).

10. The first issue of a new Internet journal specifically concerned with gender, *Intersections*, was published in 1999. This is an academic peer review forum with an anthropological basis for research and theory on the subject of gender, and the construction of gender types in different cultures.

11. Lang, S., *op. cit.*, (Chapter 6).

12. Balzer, M.M., *op. cit.* (Chapter 6).

13. Balzer, M.M., *op. cit.*

14. Hekma, G., *op. cit.*

15. Theodor De Bry, *Collections peregrinatorium in Indian Occidentalem, America*, German edition. Frankfurt, M: Bry, 1590–1634, p. xxii.

16. Balzer, M.M., *op. cit.* (Chapter 6).

17. Nanda, S., *op. cit.* (Chapter 6).

18. Besnier, N., *op. cit.*

19. Dekker, R. M. and van der Pol, L.C., *The Tradition of Female Transvestism in Early Modern Europe*, translated from the Dutch by Judy Marcuse and Lotte van der Pol. London: Macmillan, 1989.

20. Although transgendered groups in some countries (e.g. Thailand, India and Polynesia) appear in the past to have specialised in public entertainment, while those in other countries (e.g. North America, Indonesia and the Philippines) have served a function in the community as spirit mediums, it is worth remarking that both these roles involve a degree of performance. The negation of persona and gender might be considered to facilitate both possession by a spirit and the taking on of a role.

21. Andaya, L.Y., *op. cit.*, (Chapter 6).

22. Gutiérrez, R.A., *When Jesus Came the Corn Mothers Went Away: Marriage, Sexuality and Power in New Mexico, 1500–1846*. Stanford: Stanford University Press, 1991.

Chapter 10: Daeng's Story

1. There are various 'cocktails' of these hormones. This particular combination is a popular one. 'Exactly what hormones are available? What Are the Details on Popularity. Dosage, Availability, Contraindications, Adverse Effects, Etc.?' *http://www.savina.com/confluence/hormone/m2f/exactly.htm* (2001)

2. At the time of writing this venue remains closed and empty. One of the original signs, 'Fascination', can still be seen in front of the steps leading up to the old theatre.

3. The reputation of several of these clinics has grown over recent years. They now attract candidates for SRS from Europe and America.

Chapter 11: Some Facts, Figures and Observations

1. See section on tallness in Chapter 3.
2. 'Exactly what hormones are available . . .' *op. cit.* (Chapter 10)
3. One doctor I interviewed was of the opinion that if the hormones which were taken had any effect on the person's height it would be to make them shorter rather than taller.
4. Figures supplied by doctors and executives of SRS clinics in Bangkok.
5. As used by Dr Preecha Tiewtranon, Bangkok Nursing Home Hospital.
6. A Thai man's identity as the male protagonist in a sexual relationship (indeed as a man, generally) is defined less in terms of the physical characteristics of his partner than by his taking on of the dominant (i.e. active) role in such a relationship. (Jackson, P. A., *op. cit.*, Chapter 5).

Chapter 12: Malee's Story

1. It is not uncommon for *kathoey* working in respectable professions, including the dancers in the more prestigious cabaret venues, to have relationships with Thai men.

Chapter 13: Kathoey and this Religious Order

1. A quote from an interview with one of the professors at Chiang Mai University.
2. Pali – *nibbana*, from the Sanskrit *nirvana*.
3. Jackson has proposed a different (though not necessarily incompatible) structural role for *kathoey* in Thai society. He suggests they provide an image against which Thai males contrast themselves in order to define their masculinity. 'If within patriarchal cultures a male's masculinity is defined relationally with respect to other males, rather than with respect to females, then it can be seen that the *kathoey* is pivotal to the construction of Thai masculinity.' Jackson, P. A., *op. cit.* (Chapter 5).

Chapter 14: Changing Attitudes – East and West

1. *Journal of Gender Studies* and *Intersections* are examples of two new academic journals that appeared in the late 1990s.

2. Kürti, L., 'Eroticism, Sexuality, and Gender Reversal in Hungarian Culture', in Ramet, S. (ed.), *op. cit.* (Chapter 3).

3. Schleiner, W., 'Cross-Dressing, Gender Errors, and Sexual Taboos in Renaissance Literature', in Ramet, S. (ed.), *op. cit.* (Chapter 3).

4. Psychologist and historian Norman Dixon has put forward a theory of how the regimes in these places tended to produce a class of military leader with a specific type of personality deficiency that would lead them consistently to make a particular kind of error in their military judgements (Dixon, N. F., *On the Psychology of Military Incompetence*, London: Jonathan Cape, 1967.)

5. An interesting account of these associations in boys' public schools is provided in Michael Campbell's novel. *Lord Dismiss Us*, London: Heinemann, 1967.

6. An initiative of the Thai tourist authorities in the late 1990s.

7. Allyn, E., *Trees in the Same Forest: Thailand's Culture and Gay Subculture (The Men of Thailand Revisted)*. San Francisco: Bua Luang Books, 1991. See also Jackson, P.A., *op. cit.* (Chapter 5) for a discussion of the relationship between *kathoey* and gay in Thailand.